FOOD
AND
FEAST
IN TUDOR
ENGLAND

The Leigh Cup, an example of the magnificent plate owned by wealthy households in the sixteenth century. It is hallmarked for the year 1513 and was presented to the Mercers' Company in 1571 by Sir Thomas Leigh expressly for use at the election of the Master of the Company. (Reproduced by courtesy of the Mercers' Company)

FOOD AND FEAST

IN TUDOR ENGLAND

ALISON SIM

SUTTON PUBLISHING

First published in the United Kingdom in 1997 by
Sutton Publishing Limited · Phoenix Mill
Thrupp · Stroud · Gloucestershire · GL5 2BU

British Library Cataloguing in Publication Data
A catalogue record for this book is available from the British Library.

ISBN 0-7509-1476-9

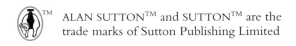
ALAN SUTTON™ and SUTTON™ are the
trade marks of Sutton Publishing Limited

Typeset in 11/14 Garamond
Typesetting and origination by
Sutton Publishing Limited.
Printed in Great Britain by
Butler & Tanner, Frome, Somerset.

*For my Dad, Alex Sim – a dreadful cook
but a wonderful father*

Contents

Contents

List of Illustrations

Acknowledgements

Thanks to Dr David Gaimster of the British Museum for his help with the tableware section.

Thanks also to the following people: Margaret Peach, Caroline Johnson and Roy Porter, whose portrayal of Henry VIII is an inspiration to us all. Thanks to Tim Massa for his advice on the wine section. Finally, thanks to Liz Clarke for providing the only B&B in London with hot and cold running gin.

CHAPTER ONE

Introduction: Food and Society in the Sixteenth Century

Sixteenth-century society revolved around the monarch. He or she could provide jobs, pensions, help in a lawsuit and just about anything else any ambitious person could want. The monarch was not an easy person to gain access to, though, so for most people it was necessary to procure the good favour of one of the charmed circle of courtiers who were regularly in the royal presence. If you wanted to move in the highest circles, you had to find ways of gaining and keeping the support of these people.

At this time it was becoming possible for individuals not born to wealth and influence to rise in the world as never before. The expansion of both trade and government bureaucracy meant that new opportunities were opening up for those able to get an education. More and more people were trying to rise in the world, and, in the process, gain influence among those close to the king or queen. An ambitious Tudor would try to dazzle the influential with a very obvious display of wealth so as to be accepted into their circle. Tudor tastes were not subtle: if you had money, you flaunted it.

The reason behind this was the strict social hierarchy that existed in Tudor times. The Tudors saw society as being rather like a ladder, with each person standing on a different rung. This ladder included not only humanity itself, but the whole of Creation, with animals, plants, minerals, etc. all having their own place on the ladder *beneath* man, and with saints, heavenly beings and, of course, God himself *above* man.

The situation was not as fixed as it might seem, though. Just as in any age, some once-powerful families found themselves going down the ladder while new families replaced them. There were also lots of people fighting at all levels over who should take precedence. Putting on a lavish display of your wealth not only confirmed your place on the ladder, it could also help you and your family to climb.

For example, the more people you employed, the more patronage you evidently had at your disposal. If you were very obviously wealthy, families higher up the social ladder might consider marrying their children to yours, which would give you access to that family's network of contacts. As most business was generated by knowing the right people, new contacts could bring you all sorts of opportunities, from jobs at Court to the chance to make sure that a judge who was trying a case you were involved in saw things your way.

Then, as now, there were plenty of other ways of showing off your wealth. The most obvious was to dress well. Before the Industrial Revolution, cloth was, in real terms, vastly more expensive than it is today. The Petre accounts, which cover the years 1548 to 1561, include London russet at 7s 4d a yard, broad russet at 2s 6d an ell and kersey from 1s 3d to 4s a yard, depending on the quality.[1] These were hardwearing, high-quality wools which wealthy people might give to their servants to wear as Sunday best or which might make an everyday gown for a merchant's wife.

It is difficult to estimate how much cloth would be needed to make a gown as there was no standard width for material at the time. Some were very narrow indeed, such as silks which might be only 22 inches wide. Gowns also varied a great deal in the amount of fabric needed. A gown for a wealthy lady who might want long, dangling sleeves and a train, if these happened to be in fashion, obviously required much more fabric than a poorer person's more practical clothes. A rough estimate of 10 yards per gown will give a fair idea, however, and it soon becomes obvious just how expensive clothing was. Considering that a skilled worker such as a shipwright might earn £12 in a year, while someone at the bottom of society, like a washerwoman, might survive on only £2, clothing formed a large part of most people's annual budget.

If you wished to display your wealth, the best fabrics to wear were silk, velvet (which was woven at least partly of silk) and even cloth of silver or gold. Not only were these fabrics expensive, they did not last as long as wool, so wearing them was a sign that you could afford to replace them as necessary. In real terms, clothes made of these fabrics cost even more than designer-original clothes cost today. John Johnson, a wealthy merchant of the staple at Calais in the mid-sixteenth century, had a quilted yellow silk doublet made up in Antwerp for a friend at the huge cost of 33s 6d – more or less a labourer's entire annual income.[2] The Tudors took dressing to impress very seriously indeed.

Ladies and gentlemen who dressed so expensively also wanted their houses to provide a magnificent setting. Tudor tastes in decoration were elaborate to say the least. Every inch of the grander rooms in a large house would be decorated with wall paintings or panelling (which would be painted in bright colours rather than lovingly polished, as surviving Tudor panelling usually is today) and, if the family was particularly wealthy, hung with tapestries. Tapestry really was the ultimate wall covering, as it would take a team of skilled weavers around three years to make a single tapestry of fairly complex design, and on top of that was the cost of all the raw materials, such as fine silk and wool thread dyed in expensively bright colours. The cost of them was enormous. Henry VIII paid £1,500 for one set of ten tapestries showing the life of King David,[3] and these were not even the best set he owned. The most magnificent in his collection were woven entirely of silk and even had silver-gilt thread woven into them. They are still on display at Hampton Court Palace.

Another necessity for the up-and-coming Tudor was a good display of plate for the table. It was still usual in the sixteenth century for guests to bring their own cutlery; huge matching sets of silver cutlery lay some way in the future. This was one reason for giving a silver spoon as a christening gift: it was a useful item which could be used throughout the recipient's life. Instead, the Tudors bought elaborate plates, bowls, ewers and other large items. Some were meant for use, others purely for display, but it was all a sound investment: if the family suddenly needed cash, the plate could be melted down and made into coin.

Certainly the Tudors were prepared to pay large amounts for their tableware. John Johnson paid the vast sum of £11 for six silver goblets which he bought in Antwerp and he also ordered no less than £40 worth of tableware for his much wealthier landlord, Sir Thomas Blundell.[4] William Harrison, in his *Description of England* (1587), describes the houses of the wealthier classes as follows: 'Certes in noblemen's houses it is not rare to see abundance of arras, rich hangings of tapestry, silver vessel, and so much other plate as may furnish sundry cupboards to the sum oftentimes of a thousand or two thousand pounds at the least, whereby the value of this and the rest of their studd doth grow to be almost inestimable. Likewise in the houses of knights, gentlemen, merchantmen and some other wealthy citizens, it is not geason to behold generally their great provision of tapestry Turkey work, pewter, brass, fine linen and thereto costly cupboards of plate, worth five or six hundred or a thousand pounds to be deemed by estimation.'[5] Plate was a vital status symbol.

Not surprisingly, feasting was a favourite pastime. Dining has always been an excellent way to impress, as it allows the host to show off not only his house and tableware but also to provide his guests with suitably expensive delicacies. The Tudors also used feasts as a way of reminding everyone where they stood in the social hierarchy. Seating was strictly according to status. The most important diners sat on the high table at one end of the hall, set up on a raised dais to put them literally at a higher level than everyone else. They would sit at one side of the table only, facing down the hall towards the other guests. The other tables would be set at right angles to the top table, with diners sitting at both sides of each table. The guests who had not quite made it on to the top table were placed at the top of the table to the right of the top table, and the order of precedence then moved down the hall, the lowest position being the bottom of the table to the far left of the top table. This strict observance of precedence must have been a nightmare for the steward and the ushers who had to organize the seating. The Tudors felt so strongly about precedence that you could create an enemy by seating someone in a place which they felt to be too lowly. The Tudors also worked very much as families rather than as individuals so you could find yourself having offended a whole family by making a mistake.

It was for this reason that the etiquette books of the time go into such detail as to who should sit where. One of these books, John Russell's *Book of Nurture,* gives such great detail about precedence that it even includes a careful list of how different bishops should be seated, and even tells you what to do with the Pope's foster parents, although it was highly unlikely that such people would visit England.[6] Diners in their turn also had to be careful not to sit down until shown to a place, as being asked to move down the table to a more lowly place would be a public humiliation.

Your place at table also determined what you were given to eat. Any modern hostess who gave some of her guests expensive dishes like quail and smoked salmon while serving others sausage and mash would be unlikely to have many people coming back a second time. In the sixteenth century, such an arrangement would be considered quite normal. The guests at the top table would be served expensive delicacies, which may also be passed on to the guests at the top of the next highest table as a sign of favour. Lower down the hall the food would be far plainer, although it was a matter of pride even so to

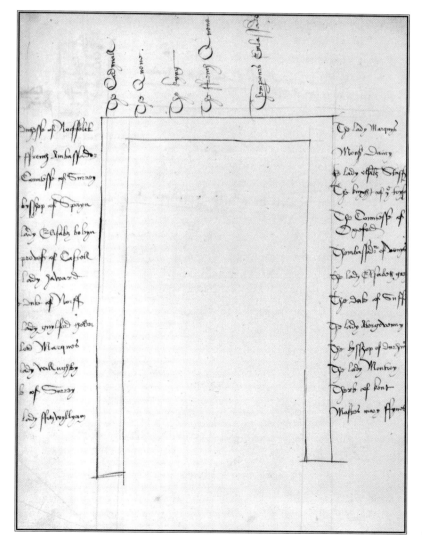

Getting the etiquette right was a vital part of entertaining. In the days when society was much more rigid than today precedence was everything, and lasting offence could be given by getting the seating arrangements wrong. Here is the seating plan for a royal banquet given at Greenwich on 7 July 1517. (College of Arms MS M8 f65v)

provide far more food than the guests could eat. Although these arrangements sound odd to us today, at the time they were considered a perfectly reasonable way of reminding everyone of their place.

The vital importance of food as an item of display can be seen from its place in the sumptuary laws. Laws trying to limit ownership of certain luxurious items to the upper social classes had existed for some time. It is hard to know how strictly they were enforced, and certainly there are many examples of these laws being ignored. The fact that they were re-enacted so often does show that the ruling classes at least took them seriously.

These laws focus on clothing but food was also covered by the sumptuary laws active during Henry VIII's reign. For example, the regulations passed on 31 May 1517 stated that a cardinal may have nine dishes served at one meal, a duke, archbishop, marquis, earl or bishop could have seven, lords 'under the degree of an earl', mayors of the city of London, knights of the garter and abbots could have six, and so on down until those with an income of between £40 and £100 a year could have three dishes. There are also strict definitions of what was meant by a 'dish' and the sheer amount of food is quite a surprise to the modern diner. A 'dish' meant one swan, bustard, peacock or 'fowls of like greatness', or four plovers, partridge, woodcock or similar birds (except in the case of a cardinal, who was allowed six), eight quail, dotterels, etc. and twelve very small birds such as larks.

Rich people's tables must have been groaning with food as there were only certain items which were restricted. Dishes such as pottages and dishes made of offal or oysters, which so cheap at this time that they were not considered to be delicacies, were not covered by the law.[7] Anyone could eat as many of these dishes as they had the money and inclination to.

There were times when the sumptuary laws could be ignored, notably at weddings, and when entertaining nobles and ambassadors, when lavish meals would be seen as honouring an important guest. If you were entertaining someone of higher degree than yourself you were allowed to dine according to the higher person's estate.

This need to impress naturally affected the cooking of the period. Cookery books of the time go into long and loving detail about how to make dishes into elaborate shapes. For example, a pig's stomach is filled with ground pork and spices and covered all over with blanched almonds so as to look like a hedgehog. A fabulous beast, the cockentrice, could be made by sewing the hind part of a pig to the front half of a capon. Dishes like these would have been sure to amuse and impress as they were paraded around before being served.[8]

The sumptuary laws give a good indication of the kind of money being spent on food by the upper classes. It seems that the wealthy were supposed to limit their spending to about 10 per cent of the value of their property. For example persons with goods to the value of £2,000 were told to limit their spending on their table to £200 a year. This is for food for their private table only, and does not include food for their household!

All this emphasis on display suggests that the Tudor's wealthier subjects lavished money on their kitchens without thought. Their entertaining was designed to give this impression but in fact expenditure was carefully controlled. Expenditure, even in the royal kitchens, was carefully supervised, and studies of other wealthy people's accounts show that they, too, kept a careful note of what was going on in their kitchens. The ninth earl of Northumberland's accounts for example show that such detailed records were kept that a note was even made of how many loaves were used at each meal.[9]

The elaborate meals you might be served at the top table in a grand palace were very unlike the everyday food that most Tudor subjects ate. The first thing that would strike most modern people about it was how boring it was. Today we take a very wide choice of food for granted, but in the sixteenth century anything imported was expensive. Ordinary people's food consisted of what could be grown locally, which meant eating the same thing day in, day out. For most Tudors a meal meant bread and pottage unless there was some kind of celebration going on.

In his *Dyetary* published in 1542 Andrew Boorde, one of Henry VIII's doctors, described pottage as being made with meat stock. In this he showed himself to be a wealthy man, as for most people meat was a treat eaten only a few times a week, or at celebrations of one kind or another. For most of the population pottage was a cross between porridge and stew, consisting of vegetables and a grain to thicken it, which was usually either oats or barley.

Different things could be added to pottage to vary the flavour, but ordinary people were limited to home-grown items like onions, leeks, garlic and herbs. Imported spices were far beyond most people's pocket. To give an idea of just how expensive they were, at the Field of Cloth of Gold, the magnificent meeting between Henry VIII and the French king Francis I in 1520, the estimated cost of food for the king, queen and nobles for a month was £7,409. Of this £440 was the estimated cost of spices alone.[10] Tudor food today has a reputation for being heavily spiced, but this can only ever have been true for the food served to the tiny minority.

Meat did sometimes appear in pottage, as Andrew Boorde's comments suggest, but meat was a luxury in most homes. It was usual for anyone who could afford it to keep a pig which would provide the family with meat for the year, but obviously this would not go very far. The meat would be preserved by being salted or smoked, so fresh meat would be unusual for most of the year for many people.

A great quantity of bread was eaten at the time. It is not always possible to be precise about the exact amount, as the best source for this information is the financial accounts of the wealthy households. All great households baked their own bread and their loaves did not necessarily conform to the official weights and measures which applied to loaves made for sale. In Dame Alice de Brynne's accounts, dating from the early fifteenth century, at least one white loaf per person, and usually more, is consumed at each meal.[11]

Poor people's bread was usually brown. Today in Britain we import most of our wheat used for bread making, as our wheat does not contain much gluten, the elastic protein that catches the gas that the yeast gives off as it works, making the bread rise. Modern bread-making methods also make our bread lighter still. Tudor bread would have been a great deal more solid than today's factory-made bread.

At all levels of society, bread was eaten, though the main ingredient would differ. Wheat was considered the finest flour for bread making, but bread was often made from other grains, such as barley, or from a mixture of grains, known as maslin. The poorest bread, made of ground-up beans, was known as horse bread as its usual use was to feed horses. Those at the bottom of the social ladder might also find themselves eating it.

Higher up the social scale food became more varied and elaborate, although the basic bread and pottage appeared even on the grandest tables. A wealthy man's pottage might contain almonds, spices and wine. One recipe book of the time, now in the British Museum, describes a pottage which was to be served cold, and which contained almonds, wine, ginger, cinnamon and saffron.[12] This was obviously a world away from the poor man's version, and would have been just one of many dishes served rather than the mainstay, but it was still basically pottage.

The rich also ate bread. At Court even the grandest people were served brown bread, but unlike most people they were also served the prestige white bread of the time, manchet. This white bread was expensive for two reasons. First, it took time to make. The brown flour had to be sifted through a fine linen cloth to remove the bran. Secondly, it was not as filling as brown bread, so it was a way of showing that you could afford to eat plenty of other things as well.

The higher up society you were the more meat you would expect to eat. It has been estimated that 80 per cent of the diet of Henry VIII's courtiers consisted of meat.[13] Rich people were also able to enjoy fresh meat all year round. They could afford to keep animals alive during the winter and kill them when required and, of course, their frequent hunting expeditions provided plenty of fresh game. In towns the better-off could also buy fresh meat from the butchers, who slaughtered animals all year round.

The rich could afford to eat sugar, too. We take this very much for granted today but in the sixteenth century this was a luxury item, beyond the pocket of most of the population. At the beginning of the sixteenth century this cost 3*d* a pound, at a time when the average semi-skilled labourer was earning 4*d* a day. By the 1540s it had gone up to 9*d* or 10*d* a pound. John Johnson paid 6*s* 6*d* for a sugar loaf for his wife Sabine,[14] which even at Court is not recorded as having been served to any but the upper courtiers. This is one reason why confectionery was such a prized skill, the sort of art that young ladies were taught as a sign of good upbringing.

The king's confectioners were expected to produce many creations which demanded not only technical skill, but also considerable artistic ability. Since the Middle Ages, the highlight of each course at a feast had been a subtlety. This consisted of some kind of sugar creation, made of sugar paste or marchpane (marzipan), which would be relevant to the occasion. For example, when William Warham was enthroned as Archbishop of Canterbury in 1505, among the subtleties presented was the interior of an abbey church, complete with various altars.[15] These works of art would be paraded around so that all the guests could admire the skill of the confectioners, and, by implication, the wealth of the host.

The wide variety of fruit illustrated in John Parkinson's *Paradisi in Sole* demonstrates that there was great interest in producing fruit for the table. The plate here shows various types of apricots and peaches. (Guildhall Library, Corporation of London)

The Tudors were concerned with healthy eating, as is shown by the dietary manuals printed in the sixteenth century, but their ideas as to what was healthy and what was not were very different from our own. It is often said that wealthy Tudors did not eat fruit and vegetables, but that statement needs to be qualified. Vegetables were generally poor men's food, but that did not mean that the rich never ate them. Fruit also reached even the highest of tables. Certain fruits, such as cherries and strawberries, were enjoyed at all levels of society, but they had a far shorter season than today. Much of the imported fruit that we now take for granted was, of course, completely unknown in England at the time. Fruit which did survive the long sea journey, like oranges and lemons, was a very expensive luxury.

The range and availability of fruit did begin to improve in the sixteenth century, however. There was an increased interest in gardening and new varieties began to be imported from the Continent. Harrison comments in 1587 that a wider range of plums was available than ever before, and W. Turner, writing in 1548, talks of apricots growing in England, although they are obviously new to him.[16] Peaches were certainly being grown at the time, though not many varieties. However, by the time Thomas Johnson revised John Gerard's *Herball* in 1633 several varieties were mentioned. Supplies of less exotic fruit, too, were improving. In 1597 Gerard includes several varieties of apple in *Herball*[17] and John Parkinson,[18] writing in 1629, even states that so many different types were grown that it was impossible to name them all. Parkinson also makes the following observation: 'The best sorts of Apples serve at the last course for the table, in most men's houses of account; where, if there grow any rare or excellent fruit, it is then set forth to be seene and tasted.'

Fruit, therefore, was obviously valued even by the wealthy. Given its limited availability, however, fresh fruit cannot have enjoyed the central place in most people's diets that it does today. Much of the fruit that was grown must have ended up being preserved in some form, as a good housewife always had to have the winter at the back of her mind. Household manuals of the time are full of instructions on how to preserve almost anything that grows, from soft fruit to rose petals.

Vegetables certainly were eaten by the wealthy, in the form of 'sallats'. These were not quite like modern salads, as they contained cooked and preserved items as well as fresh ones. They also included a variety of herbs and flowers such as violets and cowslips, which would not generally be used in salads today. This is what Gervase Markham has to say about sallats in *The English Housewife*, first published in 1615:

> First then to speak of sallats, there be some simple, and some compounded; some only to furnish out the table, and some both for use and adornation: your simple sallats are chibols [a type of mild onion] peeled, washed clean, and half of the green tops cut clean away, so served on a fruit dish; or chives, scallions, radish roots, boiled carrots, skirrets [a type of water parsnip], and turnips, with such like served up simply; also, all young lettuce, cabbage lettuce, purslane and divers other herbs which may be served simply without anything but a little vinegar, sallat oil, and sugar; onions boiled, and stripped from their rind and served up with vinegar, oil and pepper is a good simple sallat; so is samphire, bean cods [bean pods], asparagus, and cucumbers, served likewise with oil, vinegar, and pepper, with a world of others too tedious to mention.[19]

Salads were often highly decorative, with the vegetables carved into a variety of elaborate shapes. Markham even includes instruction on making 'sallats for show only'. These consist of carrot roots of various colours (there were at least four varieties of carrot available at the time, all of different colours) carved into 'many shapes and proportions, as some into knots, some in the matter of scutcheons and arms, some like birds, and some like wild beasts, according to the art and cunning of the workman . . .'[20]

Other sallats were made for eating, and for eating by even the very grandest. Markham describes how to make one elaborate sallat intended to be served at a grand meal, commenting that such a dish 'is usual at great feasts, and upon princes' tables'. The salad he suggests for this use contains almonds, raisins, capers, olives, currants, red sage and spinach, all mixed together with a 'good store of sugar'. This is put into a dish, with vinegar and oil, and yet more sugar. Thin slices of oranges and lemons are then laid over this, so as to cover it, followed by a layer of red cauliflower leaves, a layer of olives, a layer of 'well-pickled' cucumber, then a layer of the shredded heart of a cabbage lettuce. The sallat is topped with another layer of orange and lemon slices.

This hall house from the Weald and Downland Museum was probably built some time in the fifteenth or early sixteenth century. It had a hall for the household and originally had a separate room, sealed off from the hall, for the family. (Weald and Downland Open Air Museum/Alison Sim)

Another, much simpler, sallat given by Markham would not be considered a salad at all today, but would simply count as a cooked vegetable. This consists of spinach, first well boiled and then put into a pot with butter and boiled again. Currants are then added, and 'as much vinegar as will make it reasonable tart', and then it is seasoned with sugar 'according to the taste of the master of the house'. It is then served upon 'sippets' (toasted or fried slices of bread). It is clear that even the well-to-do were happy to eat vegetables.

Flowers of various kinds seem to have been greatly used in sallats, as Markham mentions them several times and even gives a recipe for preserving flowers in sugar and vinegar for use in sallats. Great attention was paid to the appearance of food at the time, and doubtless the flowers were very useful in decorating the dishes. Certainly the housewife is instructed to use distilled vinegar so that the flowers will keep their colour better.[21]

The various pickles described by Markham obviously were sometimes served up simply in a dish, as they are characterized as being 'good and dainty' served in this way. However, the complicated instructions given for making decorated sallats suggest that these must have been quite a feature at a more formal meal, although the taste of them was also appreciated. One set of instructions for an elaborately decorated sallat ends with the assurance that 'these sallats are both for show and use, for they are more excellent to taste than to look on'.

This farmhouse was built in the late sixteenth century and contrasts with the Boarhunt Hall. It would have been built for a yeoman farmer (i.e. one who owned his own land) as the Boarhunt Hall would have been. The two show how conditions changed in the sixteenth century. The yeomanry were doing well and this house was built without a hall. Instead it had upstairs and downstairs rooms heated by a massive central chimney. The kitchen was built as part of the house rather than as a separate building. (Weald and Downland Open Air Museum/Alison Sim)

At the lower end of society cooking was basic, requiring only a small number of pots and utensils. This had to be the case: manufactured goods were expensive so many households had only a bare minimum of equipment. At the grander end, however, cooking and serving the great variety of dishes required was skilled work. Often the woman of the house would have to do the cooking, helped by her servants. Unless they were very wealthy indeed, Tudor households did not have the huge numbers of servants enjoyed by the wealthier Victorians, so this was hard work. Servants were also treated rather differently in a Tudor household, in that they were people you worked alongside rather than people whom you regarded as inferiors, so that entertaining for most Tudor women was not just a matter of organizing a menu with the staff and waiting for the food to appear.

In a very big household, such as that of a great duke or of the king himself, an army of staff was required to feed the large numbers of people involved. Henry VIII employed around two hundred people in his kitchens and they had to produce about six hundred covers twice a day. These large kitchens had to be as highly organized as any kitchen in a grand hotel today.[22]

Tudor dining, at least for the wealthier section of the population, was much more sophisticated than is generally believed. It involved great skill on the part of everyone from the cooks to the gold- and silversmiths who made the elaborate plate used. The diners, too, would have been very well behaved, being keen to show off their good manners. Despite the lack of forks, they would have eaten with a delicacy that would surprise most modern people. It was all a world away from the riotous dining shown in most films depicting the Tudors.

CHAPTER TWO

Kitchens and Kitchen Equipment

Kitchens in the sixteenth century varied according to people's lifestyles and income just as they do today. At the top end of the range were the huge, well-equipped kitchens of royalty and the nobility, but at the other end of the social scale houses might well have no kitchen at all. Fuel for fires was expensive, so all the cooking would be done over the fire in the main room, meaning that there was no separate kitchen. Kitchen equipment varied too. At the bottom end of the scale it was very basic, while the great kitchens of the wealthy required all manner of fancy equipment, such as the elaborate moulds needed for confectionery work.

The task of reconstructing a kitchen of the time demands a mixture of archaeology and the study of documents. Fortunately a number of inventories survive, listing the contents of people's houses. These do have their limitations. Firstly, they were only made for those with moveable goods worth over £5, which excluded quite a few people. Secondly, it is likely that articles of very little value were left out. Pottery probably often fell into this category. The fact that relatively few pottery articles are found in such lists gives the impression that little pottery was used, when in fact archaeological surveys uncover large quantities of it.

The most basic need in the kitchen was a fire. This was usually a wood fire, although furze, straw, turf or peat might also be used. Another option was coal, but it was often expensive. In the Royal Household coal was reserved for the fires in the private lodgings of the monarch and his immediate family. In places where coal was the most convenient fuel ranges might be used, such as one mentioned in

Durham in 1525–6.[1] These were raised iron fire baskets, a world away from the elaborate ranges produced in the late eighteenth and nineteenth centuries.

A wood fire burns best when it is elevated to allow free circulation of air, so fire dogs were used to lift the logs off the ground. They were also sometimes employed as supports for spits. When used this way they were known as cob irons. The hooks to support the spits hung from their front faces. Sometimes the front faces had a little place for a small bowl or cup at the top so that things could be kept warm by the fire.[2]

The back wall of the fireplace was very vulnerable as it was constantly being heated and then allowed to cool. The changes in temperature could cause the brickwork to split, so iron firebacks came into use. They were useful because they also helped to reflect the heat of the fire back into the room. Surviving ones are often very elaborately decorated.

Bayleaf Farmstead at the Weald and Downland Museum. This is an early fifteenth-century house, but it was still being lived in in the sixteenth century. This would have been lived in by someone moderatley well-to-do, although it did not have a brick chimney-stack and wall-mounted fireplace until 1636. Instead, it was heated with an open fire in the hall.

Some cooking may have been done over the open fire but by the sixteenth century the house probably had a separately built kitchen as well. (Weald and Downland Open Air Museum/Alison Sim)

Fires had to be handled carefully if they were not to get out of control, particularly as even in the sixteenth century many houses were still built of wood. Relighting the fire from scratch every morning was a tedious job so it was usual to rake the live embers together before the household went to bed and to cover them with a pottery fire cover. There is a very handsome example in the British Museum.

Metal obviously stood up to being heated better than pottery, so metal pots were used for cooking when the pot was going to be exposed to high heat for long periods. The metal used was generally either iron or brass (i.e. some kind of copper alloy). A metal pot is manifestly heavy and difficult to handle, especially when hot, so various equipment was needed for keeping the pot in place over the fire and for helping the cook to bring it off the heat easily. Sometimes this was a metal pot hook which would be suspended from the cross-beam in the chimney, and sometimes a more sophisticated crane was used, which would be attached to the wall. This had a hinged bar, allowing the pot to be swung on and off the fire. There is also evidence that both pot hooks and cranes might be used within the same household, as both were included in the contents of a cellar at the time of a fire in Norwich in 1507.[3]

Most people associate cooking over open fires with huge metal cauldrons, but cookery books of the time and inventories demonstrate a large range of metal pots, especially in wealthy people's kitchens where elaborate cooking went on. Kettles, which were either round-bellied, like small cauldrons, or flat-bottomed and which were designed to hang over a fire, were general-purpose items used for boiling. In his instructions for making a Spanish dish of boiled meat called *olla podrida* Gervase Markham advises the housewife to 'take a very large vessel, pot or kettle . . .'[4] as the standard way of boiling. Boiling meat was such a standard process that large kitchens often came with a built-in boiler to boil meat and make stock. This would be set over a furnace, or brick-enclosed fire, like the ones used for making beer. Often they were huge: the copper in the Hampton Court kitchen, which has been restored, holds about 75 gallons.[5]

Metal pots and pans were not all designed to be suspended over the fire. Some were designed instead to be rested on trivets or grid-irons. Saucepans could be used this way. They were very like modern saucepans except that the handle was longer, to allow the cook to distance himself or herself from the heat of the fire. Frying pans also had long handles, for the same reason. One type of pot-bellied pot, called a posnet, had a handle and could be used in the same way, although it also had three little legs to allow it to stand directly among the coals of the fire if necessary.

Some types of cookery required a more moderate heat than the full force of the fire. Delicate sauces and confectionery required a gentle and constant heat, for which the most suitable fuel was charcoal. In large kitchens special stoves might be built for the purpose. These were very like a modern barbecue, built into stone work-surfaces. They had permanent metal grids set over the top, on which to balance the cooking vessel, and a vent beneath for the ash to fall into. A very impressive stove with five such 'barbecues' was built into the Hampton Court kitchen in the seventeenth century. It still survives today.[6]

A permanent stove was not always appropriate, and delicate work could also be done with a chafing dish. A dish of either metal or earthenware would be used to hold either charcoal or live coals, and the saucepan or chafing dish could either be supported on a tripod or suspended in some way over the heat. This arrangement was often used by ladies for their confectionery work.

It was not only delicate sauces that required more gentle heat. Food might need to be kept warm, and this could be achieved by putting the food in an earthenware pot and placing it among the coals of the fire. Another pot-bellied pot, called a pipkin, was often used for this purpose. John Murrell talks of a 'green pipkin' in a recipe for boiling chicken in his *Two Books of Cookery and Carving*.[7] This was probably the pottery known as 'Tudor greenware', to be discussed in chapter seven, because, as Stuart Peachy points out, a green glaze made of verdigris on a copper pot would have been useless.[8] Some pipkins were evidently quite large as Markham describes a recipe in which a lamb's 'purtenance' is boiled in one. The 'purtenance' consisted of the head, heart, lights, liver and windpipe.[9]

Pottery was sometimes used for moulds which were intended to be broken. For example, in one fifteenth-century recipe called 'Appraylere' cooked pork was to be ground up and cheese, breadcrumbs and spices added; then the mixture was bound together with egg. This would all be packed into a pitcher. Canvas was then wrapped securely around the pitcher to keep the mixture together and it was put into a cauldron to boil. Once the meat was cooked, the pitcher was broken so the meat could be removed in one piece. The final stage was to put this meat on a spit and roast it. After that it was covered with spiced batter before finally being served.[10]

This brings us to the type of cooking that most people associate with Tudor kitchens, namely spit-roasting meat. It was possible to roast meat before a fire without a spit, using a skein of worsted suspended from a hook. The thread would be twisted up tightly so that it unwound slowly, turning the meat.[11] This would only be suitable for a small piece of meat, but as meat was a luxury for most people this was not a problem.

Meat could also be roasted by toasting it before the fire, either on a fork of some kind or suspended from a plate of iron with hooks in it. Markham describes both these methods of cooking.[12] As with all roasting, a dish would be placed under the meat to catch the juices, which would later be made up into sauce to accompany the meat. Although it was quite possible to manage without a spit, even humble kitchens often contained one. For example, in 1660 John David ap John, an ordinary farmer who lived at Llanfair, owned a spit.[13]

Roasting meat on a spit looks deceptively simple, but as anyone who has ever tried it will know, good preparation and careful supervision of the meat are both required. Here are Markham's observations on the process:

> To proceed then to roast meats, it is to be understood that in the general knowledge thereof are to be observed these few rules. First, the cleanly keeping and scouring of the spits and cob-irons; next the neat picking and washing of meat before it is spitted, then the spitting and broaching of the meat, which must be done so strongly and firmly that the meat may by no means either shrink from the spit or else turn about the spit: and yet ever to observe that the spit do not go through any principal part of the meat, but such as is of least account and estimation: and if it be birds of fowl which you spit, then to let the spit go through the hollow of the body of the fowl, and so fasten it with picks or skewers under the wings, about the thighs of the fowl, and at the feet or rump, according to your manner of trussing and dressing them.[14]

The temperature of the fire was another matter to consider. A cook had to be able to judge whether the fire was ready and to keep an eye on it to ensure that the fire remained at the right temperature. Different meats, of course, required different levels of heat. Swan, turkey and bustard, for example, required a slow fire while pig, pullet, pheasant and quail needed a 'quick and sharp fire'.

This scene shows a clockwork spit in use – note the counterweight hanging down by the fire. (Samantha Doty)

In a very large kitchen different fires could be used for different meats, but this was not always possible. Sometimes several different items had to be roasted in front of the same fire at the same time. This was manageable, but it took organization and care. Markham describes how to do it, giving the example of roasting a chine of beef, a loin of mutton, a capon and a lark all at the same time. The beef, as the largest item, had to be parboiled until it was about half-cooked. The capon would be loaded on to the spit next to the hand of the person turning it (who would be standing at the cooler end of the fire). The beef was placed beside the capon, the lark placed beside that and finally the mutton was put on the spit. The beef and the fat part of the mutton were to cover the lark, to keep it from burning. The capon and the loin of mutton were basted with cold water and salt, while the beef was basted with boiling lard. Once the beef was almost done it was opened to hasten the cooking process while the mutton and the capon were basted with butter until fully cooked. The lark, by this stage, would also be ready so that all the meat was ready to be served at the same time.[15]

Turning the spit was a very unpleasant job. The draught from the air that roared up the chimney combined with the heat from the fire meant that the turnspit was both boiling hot and freezing cold at the same time. It was no surprise that turning the spit was one of the first jobs to be mechanized.

By the sixteenth century dogs had already been called into service to replace humans. Dr Cauis described a turnspit dog in 1536. The dogs were trained to run inside a little treadmill which powered the spit via a pulley attached to one end of the spit. Turnspit dogs were still in use in some places in the nineteenth century.[16] However, the more usual means of turning the spit was a clockwork mechanism known as a jack. Smoke jacks existed at this time, although they really only became common in England in the eighteenth century. The smoke jack had a type of propeller called a fly, which was turned not by smoke, but by the hot air from the fire as it escaped up the chimney. This turned the spit via a gear mechanism.[17]

As bread was very much part of the staple diet at the time, some kind of oven was needed. Ovens were made of brick or stone and were dome-shaped. They were usually built into a wall, often next to the fireplace, and a fire would be lit inside. Once the oven was hot enough the fire would be raked out and then the bread, or whatever was to be cooked, would be put inside.

It was very expensive to heat an oven and so there were other, cheaper ways of baking bread. In areas where oatcakes, rather than leavened bread, tended to be eaten a bakestone was often used. This was usually made of metal rather than stone and took the form of a round plate which rested on four legs. This could be stood over the fire and the oatcakes cooked on top. The bakestone could also be used to bake leavened bread. In this case, the bread would be put under an upturned iron pot. The bakestone would be placed over it and hot coals would be built up over the pot and bakestone to make a kind of oven.

A Tudor kitchen, like any modern one, needed not only a variety of cooking equipment but also a range of items for storing food and drink. Barrels of various sizes were the standard 'packaging' of the day, providing plenty of work for the coopers who made and repaired them. They were used not only for holding wine and beer but also for such a wide variety of foods as salt fish, olives and dried fruit. John Parkinson comments in *Paradisi in Sole* that damsons dried in France were being imported into England in barrels. They were not an easy form of packaging to deal with. (Some of the trials of handling them are described in chapter five.) They were also fairly expensive – those who brewed for the Royal Household were supplied with casks which they were to use only for that purpose. If these casks were misused, there could, in theory at least, be severe consequences. Those brewers or their servants who spoiled the cask or who used them for their own purposes were liable to be discharged from brewing for the king.[18]

Wooden boxes were also used for storage, but probably only for expensive items like sweetmeats. For example, Markham talks of putting marmalade into boxes.[19] Wicker baskets were another general-purpose container; they were also useful for the general fetching and carrying of everything from coal to fruit.

Some foods had to be kept in fairly airtight conditions. A gallipot was a straight-sided earthenware jar with a rim, and as it was much more resistant to heat than a glass jar, it was a good option for storing various preserves. Large earthenware pots were also used to store clarified butter for cooking. A more short-term way of keeping air out was to use pastry. Some pastry was meant solely for eating, such as the 'puff paste' described by Markham, which was like its modern counterpart.[20] Other pastry, though, was not intended for eating. Markham advises that 'red deer venison, wild boar, gammons of bacon, swans, elks, porpoise, and such like standing dishes, which must be kept long, should be baked in a moist, thick, tough, coarse and long-lasting crust . . .' He considered that rye pastry was best for this purpose. Dishes like lamb and waterfowl, which would come to the table more than once, but not for many days, should be baked in a good white crust.[21] Pastry, therefore, would have been a cheap and convenient way of keeping the meat moist.

Another simple method of storage was simply to hang things such as smoked meat from a beam. This kept it out of the way of dogs, cats and vermin, all of which could be a problem.

Storage in a large kitchen had to be carefully thought out. On the one hand, it was not desirable for the staff to waste time because of unnecessarily long walks, so the larders had to be convenient. On the other hand, if the larders were too accessible people might be tempted to steal. The storage at Hampton Court is carefully designed so that the wet, dry and flesh larders all lead off a single court which has only one doorway.[22] This door was also designed to be locked.

Larger kitchens, like the royal kitchens, had to deal not only with large quantities of food but also with a wide variety of items which needed specialist storage. A good example was the wet kitchen, where fish was kept. Saltwater fish was brought to the household wrapped in seaweed to keep it fresh. The king would even have a sea fisher who was contracted to keep the Royal Household supplied.[23] Other fish, though, was kept alive right up to the last moment. Many houses, not just the Royal Household, had fishponds for this

The Pond Garden at Hampton Court was originally one of Henry VIII's fishponds. There were also a number of banqueting houses in the palace gardens, but none survive today. The one shown here was built for William III. (Alison Sim)

purpose; the moat of a house might also be used. Cardinal Wolsey's London palace, York Place (the building which later became Whitehall Palace), had a fish-house with piped running water where fish could be kept alive.[24]

Considerable thought was put into kitchen design generally. Andrew Boorde, in *Dyetary of Health*, describes the ideal kitchen, giving not only the layout of the kitchen and its offices but also reminding his readers that the slaughterhouse, stables, dairy, bakehouse and brewhouse should be built about a quarter of a mile from the house. This was partly because of the noise and smell of such places, but in the case of the bake- and brewhouses fire was always a hazard.[25]

In the Middle Ages kitchens were often built away from the house because of the fire hazard. For example, the kitchen at Haddon Hall, built in the fourteenth century, is a separate building, as is the fourteenth-century monastic kitchen at Durham Cathedral.[26] This began to change in the fifteenth century, and the famous sixteenth-century 'prodigy houses' all had kitchens which were firmly built in as part of the house.

The reason for this change was at least partly that of fashion. Medieval great houses had often been large, sprawling affairs but by the sixteenth century the ideas of symmetry and even the influence of classical architecture began to change things. There was a move towards hiding the less attractive areas of the house, while showing off the grander ones to greater advantage. The classical idea of a *piano nobile* was gaining prominence; that is, of literally elevating areas such as the rooms used by the owner of the house and his guests.

These two ideas could be dealt with simultaneously by building the kitchen in the basement. The support of the outside earth meant that the kitchen could be given solid stone walls and even a stone-vaulted ceiling to minimize the risk of a fire spreading to the rest of the house. At the same time the grander areas in the house could be raised away from cold and damp, to where they could enjoy the fine views so loved by the Elizabethans.[27]

Kitchens were also designed with hygiene in mind. The Tudors were aware that there was a link between dirt and disease, although of course they did not know of the existence of bacteria. They thought that the real danger lay in bad smells, as Andrew Boorde was keen to point out, but the net result was that cleanliness in the kitchen was considered important. 'And of all thynges, let the buttery, the cellar, the kytchen, the larder-house, with all other howses of offices be kept clene,'[28] he advises his readers. The wealthy person's kitchen was therefore designed to be easy to clean.

The first thing that was necessary was a good supply of water. This might be drawn from a well, but supplies of piped running water were also known. In the Middle Ages monasteries had often been built with a running water supply. A famous plan of Canterbury Cathedral's water supply executed in the twelfth century shows a system that does everything from flushing out the toilets to cooling wine in the cellar. There was even an 'emergency back-up' system for when supplies ran low.[29]

Such efficient systems were unusual even in grand houses, although not unknown. The one at Hampton Court Palace, for example, carried water from various conduit-houses at Coombe Hill, about 3 miles away. The water served the whole palace, not just the kitchens and their associated offices such as the wet-larder where fish was kept. The bathrooms in the royal lodgings had running water, and there was a 'House of Easement' which had water running through the sewers underneath to keep it clean, as recommended by Boorde.[30]

It was not only Hampton Court which was supplied in this way. Both Greenwich and Whitehall palaces had efficient water supplies. Such elaborate systems must have been a necessity, rather than a luxury, at Henry's 'great houses' where he held full court. The grand houses sometimes housed over a thousand people when the king was in residence, so there had to be ways of keeping the palace clean if the court was to stay in one place for more than a few days.

Lower down the social scale, water supply was more of a problem. In rural communities most houses would be situated near a river or a well and the heavy work of carrying water to the house would be part of everyday life. In towns, piped water did exist, but it was a luxury. Many larger and more prosperous towns had had piped water of some kind since the Middle Ages. Southampton was one such city. It benefited from an existing system. A Franciscan friary had been established there towards the end of the thirteenth century, and the friars had set up a conduit to bring water from a spring at Colewell Hill to the waterhouse which still stands on Commercial Road. Work on the conduit began in 1304 and went on for the next thirty years. In 1420 the borough bought it and it became available for public use.[31]

The Water House,
Southampton, which helped
bring running water to the
city. (Julie Anne Hudson)

The existence of a public conduit did not mean that every house in Southampton now had piped water, merely that you could fetch water from the conduit if you so wished. It took money and influence to have a private water supply piped to your house. The wealthy merchant John Fleming did negotiate such an arrangement in 1515, but in return he had to donate a spring to feed the conduit to the corporation.[32]

The Franciscans were obviously keen to have a good water supply as they also built the original of the Trinity conduit which still serves Cambridge. The original, open conduit was built in 1325, and during the fifteenth century the water also supplied the college of King's Hall, which was extended at that time. As was often the case with a water supply, the conduit was the cause of a great deal of argument between the two institutions, until the Dissolution left King's Hall the sole owner. Henry VIII then included King's Hall in his new foundation of Trinity College and the water was tapped to the kitchen of the grand new college. The water was also used by people of the town. The fountain in Trinity Great Court is still served by it.[33]

The fountain in Trinity Great Court, Cambridge. It is still served by the Trinity conduit originally built by Franciscan friars in the fourteenth century. The fountain is largely that built in 1601–2. (Alison Sim)

Disputes over water supply were common. Technically, it was illegal to tap a public conduit to supply a private house but in practice it was difficult to stop people from doing it, especially if they had powerful connections. A broadside, believed to have been published in 1612, gives some idea of just how complex water disputes could become.

This broadside takes the form of 'The humble petition of the whole companie of the poor Water-Tankerd-bearers of the Citie of London, and the Suburbs . . .' The water bearers were the people you could buy water from if you did not want to carry water from the public conduits yourself. According to them, the public water supplies were being tapped illegally to numerous private houses. Much of this plumbing work had even been done by a Mr Randall, the city's own plumber, on his own admission. Builders putting up new houses in Covent Garden had also unearthed the public water-

This part of Hampton Court originally contained the House of Ease, the multi-seater 'public' toilet at the palace. The sewers under it were constantly flushed with water. Grander courtiers also had private privies (without the flushing arrangement) in their private apartments. (Alison Sim)

pipes and tapped them to the new houses. As a result, the public conduits were running dry, threatening the water-sellers' business.[34]

Water was, of course, only one necessity for keeping the kitchen clean. Some effective means of waste disposal also had to be organized. There cannot have been a great deal of waste from a Tudor kitchen, even if the household was a very grand one. Important people expected to be served with far more food than they could eat, as a matter of status, but what they left was not thrown out. Their leavings worked their way down the social system of the household, with the high-status 'unbroken meats' which they had not even touched going to their personal servants and so on, until the food that nobody wanted was given to poor people outside the gate. The main problem, therefore, was not how to dispose of waste but the waste water generated by washing everything from pots and pans to the various floors of the offices.

Good drains were essential, especially in larger houses. Many such houses still had moats, but in the well-ordered house the drains did not empty into it. The effects of dirty water being poured constantly into the still waters of the moat would soon have made the house uninhabitable. Andrew Boorde advised that the moat of a house should be fed by a fresh spring and that the moat should also be scoured frequently to keep it clean. No kitchen waste was to be emptied into it.[35]

The drains from the kitchen at Hampton Court kept these rules. They ran down the centre of the kitchen court, to allow them to pick up waste from the various household offices, and then ran out under the moat. The flagged kitchen floor was also sloped towards the drains to allow the water to run into them easily.

It was not only royalty who were concerned with good drainage. Archaeological excavations at Southampton show that the wealthier citizens were prepared to meet the considerable cost of adequate drainage and sanitation even in the Middle Ages. Stone-lined drains, carefully sited to take advantage of the natural fall of the land, have been found dating from the thirteenth century. One drain served at least three outlets and took both sewage and kitchen waste to the sea.

A sink for disposing of waste water (reproduced from Dorothy Hartley's *Water in England*, MacDonald, 1964).

A cesspit built in the sixteenth century with a vaulted stone roof has also been found, and this must have been expensive to build.[36]

Flagged floors and piped drainage were available only to the better-off. Most ordinary people had trodden earth floors in their houses, so washing them down was not an option. There were no drains for disposing of waste water inside the house, but that did not mean that there was no system of drainage connected to such houses.

The usual way to get rid of waste water was to pour it down a sink. A sink was basically a hole in the ground. The idea was that water could gradually drain back into the surrounding earth without allowing the topsoil to become waterlogged. This remained a very efficient means of disposing of dirty water until towns became so densely populated that the soil could no longer cope with all the water.[37]

In general, Tudor kitchens were as well designed as our kitchens are today. The equipment may look primitive to us but it made good use of the technology of the time, and considering the incredible banquets produced in some kitchens the cooks knew how to make good use of it.

CHAPTER THREE

Staffing and Provisioning the Kitchen

T he staff who worked in a Tudor kitchen were very different from the staff who would have been found in a Georgian or Victorian kitchen. For one thing, the staff in a grand household were usually men. It cost more to employ male servants than female, so grand households liked to employ men as a status symbol. Women were employed to do the washing (which was always seen as a woman's job) and as casual labour for tasks such as weeding the garden. In Henry VIII's own household there was only one woman who worked in the kitchens. She worked in the confectionery, but sadly we know nothing about her.[1]

Lower down the social scale women were employed to do the cooking, but at that level they would not be specialist cooks so much as a kind of maid-of-all-work who would help out with whatever housework needed to be done. Girls were sometimes officially apprenticed to learn housewifery, although often they were taught another trade as well. For example, in Shrewsbury in 1612 Elizabeth Deacon was bound apprentice to a Salisbury tailor and his wife in 'the mistery and sciences of huswyfyrye and flaxdressing'.[2]

The servant's lot in the sixteenth century was not necessarily a bad one. There were, of course, bad employers, but in general service could be quite a good career. A servant was usually given two sets of clothing a year, which would be a livery or uniform in a grand household. Sir William Petre clothed his servants in grey frieze (a coarse woollen cloth) in the winter and grey 'marble' (a parti-coloured worsted woven to resemble the veining in marble) in the summer. As clothing was expensive, that was quite a good deal.[3]

Shoes were also provided by the master or mistress. The shoemaker charged 7*d* a pair for the Petres' children's shoes, as opposed to 9*d* for a pair for the kitchen boy. This was because the kitchen boy's shoes would have to be of tougher construction to stand harder wear.[4] Board and lodging were usually provided too, so most servants did not have to pay towards their daily living expenses.

Servants had a different relationship with their employer from the one that we are familiar with from eighteenth- and nineteenth-century novels. In most households the cook was the lady of the house, and if servants were employed there, they worked alongside her, rather than spending most of their lives hidden away behind a green baize door. The housewifery manuals of the time were obviously aimed at well-to-do women, since books were expensive. Even so grand a lady as Lady Elinor Fettiplace annotated her receipt book herself and obviously had a practical, first-hand knowledge of cookery.[5] Her work in the kitchen must have meant that she got to know her kitchen staff in a way that a Victorian lady would never have done.

Even the grandest people did not feel that their kitchen staff were there to be ignored. The Tudor monarchs all showed an interest in their household and not just in the grander staff who worked in their private apartments. Richard Hill, the sergeant of the cellar, was a frequent gambling partner of Henry VIII between 1527 and 1539.[6] This is not to say, of course, that men such as Richard Hill would have been personal friends of the king in the way that important courtiers like Charles Brandon, the Duke of Suffolk, were. The point is that the below-stairs staff were far from being considered too humble to merit royal attention.

In large households there was a very clear hierarchy in the kitchen. Kitchen staff have to work quickly, under a great deal of pressure, and so almost military discipline is necessary if everything is to reach the table on time. The clerk of the kitchen was at the top of the organization. He would have been an educated man with a great deal of work to do. It was his job to organize the provisioning of the kitchen while also keeping a close eye on the stores. He doled out the ingredients needed by the cooks, kept the keys of the various stores, and made up accounts to present either to the household steward or, in the case of the Royal Household, to the Board of the Greencloth, which was the group of men responsible for the day-to-day running of the king's Household. They did everything from checking up on the finances to maintaining discipline.[7]

Organising and provisioning a large household was a complicated job. Here is the first page of the Eltham Ordinances, drawn up by Cardinal Wolsey for running Henry VIII's household. They were drawn up in 1526 but various additions were made to them later. (Public Record Office, E36/231 f.1)

The clerk of the kitchen was a man with considerable responsibility and a good one was obviously a man to be valued. The Eltham Ordinances, which were drawn up in 1526 for the running of Henry VIII's Household, show that the royal clerks of the kitchen were certainly appreciated. Their daily diet was similar to the one given to the gentlemen who attended the king, and included beef, mutton, veal, capons, conies, pheasants, and a dish of either lamb, pigeons or chicken. They even ended their meals with tart, butter and fruit.[8]

The cook was the next most important person. He was in charge of cooking, but like a modern chef, he did only the more complicated and difficult work himself. The preparation of simple dishes and all the mundane jobs like preparing vegetables were done by junior staff.

Cooks were expected to cope with the day-to-day feeding of the household, but on grand occasions extra help was brought in. A wedding was celebrated at Sir William Petre's country house, Ingatestone Hall, in June 1552 and Sir William obviously wanted only the best. A master cook named Wilcox was brought down from London to take charge, together with four under-cooks. The feelings of Richard Cook, the Petre's normal cook, on the matter are not recorded.[9]

The Royal Household had three master cooks – one for the Household kitchen and one each in the king and queen's privy kitchens. Henry VII and Henry VIII both had French cooks in addition to the master cooks, but exactly how they fitted into the scheme of things is not clear. They were certainly not counted as part of the normal kitchen staff.[10]

Despite this, even the royal kitchen sometimes found that lavish entertaining pushed it to its limits. Extra kitchen space sometimes had to be provided even at the larger royal palaces. In 1533 the preparation for the twelfth-night banquet at Greenwich Palace required the building of a temporary working house. Henry VIII often spent Christmas at the palace and temporary boiling houses had to be erected almost every year to cope with the catering.[11]

The lavish entertainments at the Field of Cloth of Gold must have been particularly taxing for the royal kitchens, as most of the cooking there had to be done in tents. The picture painted of the event, which now hangs at Hampton Court, shows a massive round outdoor bread oven built of brick, and cooking going on inside a tent. The impressive temporary palace fortunately included offices such as pantries and cellars, while a waffery, poultry (the kitchen office that dealt with poultry), scalding house, ovens and a working house for the pastry cooks were all set up in houses nearby.[12] Extra staff were also hired, including twelve pastry cooks (who earned 20*d* a day), twelve brewers (12*d* a day) and twelve bakers (also 12*d* a day).[13] Equipment had to be hired from the cooks of London. This ranged

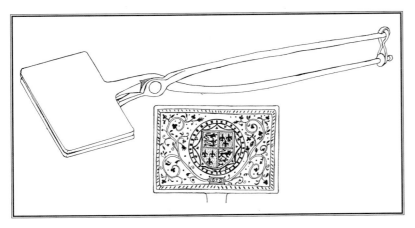

Irons such as these were used to make the wafers for wealthy people's meals. They are very similar to a modern waffle iron except that the plates were often decorated to produce patterned wafers. This one produced wafers decorated with the royal arms, engraved in reverse so as to produce a correct version on the wafer. (Samantha Doty)

from a big kettle in which to boil beef, to pots, pans and spits. The total cost of hiring such equipment was a massive £377 11s.[14]

The task of moving the entire Household across to France was probably not quite as daunting as we might think. The Royal Household lived on the move. Henry VIII usually relocated about thirty times a year, only staying for about two weeks in any one place. Likewise Queen Elizabeth was famous for her summer progresses. Moving for the royal staff was the normal state of affairs.

It was for this reason that the Royal Household had to be flexible. Not all of the palaces were huge places like Hampton Court or Whitehall. Some were deliberately designed to be small enough to allow the monarch to escape the pressure of being surrounded by people. If the monarch was at one of these palaces, only a small number of staff would actually be needed. The rest would be put on board wages until their services were required again.

The status of cooks seems to have been quite high. Sir William Petre's cook accompanied his master when he went to Boulogne and was in the Petre's pay for some years. The royal master cooks were given a diet very similar to that of the clerk of the kitchen, although they were not given the tart, butter and fruit which the clerk enjoyed.[15]

The situation for younger and less important servants, particularly the kind employed to do general housework and not just cooking, was not so favourable. The *Salisbury Easter Books* suggest that such servants usually only stayed with a family for a year or two before moving on.[16] This was more the choice of the servants than their masters. There was nothing much to be gained from staying in a household where you might be the only servant.

In a large household the situation was rather different. There were plenty of opportunities for advancement, albeit mainly for men. The bottom servants in the royal kitchen, the 'scolyones', were young boys who had the job of keeping the kitchen, courtyards and so on clean. The master cooks would be given 20 marks a year to provide the boys with decent clothing. However, according to the Eltham Ordinances they had been going either naked 'or in garments of such vilenesse' that it was positively disgusting. Life as a scullion was not easy but there were wonderful opportunities. The Ordinances state that some of these boys were to be taught to be cooks, giving them the vital entrée into the Royal Household which could be a career for life.[17]

Great households were a good place to work as they generally provided job security. The employers would often look after their servants when they could not work owing to illness. The Royal Household was the best of all. There was considerable job security, because even though the Tudors ran out of money from time to time they never reduced their Households as a result. As a royal servant, you could expect to be maintained in illness or old age, and during a temporary illness you would be paid board wages. If you were not able to work any longer for some reason you could either sell your place or be supported by the monarch in some way.

The Royal Household provided such good career opportunities that even quite important gentlemen were prepared to enter their younger sons in fairly lowly positions. Sir John Gage held the posts of controller, vice-chamberlain and lord chamberlain at different times but he was happy to see his second son James enter the Royal Household in the lowly rank of groom. James did well and was master of the Household by the time Edward VI was crowned.[18]

Perquisites were another benefit that could make service a good career. Perquisites were many and various, and in a large household could include everything from candle ends (wax candles were expensive and the ends were recycled to make new candles) to the leavings from the table of the master and mistress. This system had already enjoyed a long history even by the sixteenth century and it went on until people could no longer afford to keep large households of servants. Well into this century cooks were still allowed to keep dripping and rabbit skins, not to mention various other bits and pieces.[19] These perquisites could end up costing an employer quite a lot of money, but they were such an established right that the wise employer did not argue with them.

The kitchen gatehouse, Hampton Court. The counting house, where the Board of the Greencloth met, had their office over it. The administrative staff of the kitchen all had their rooms at first-floor level in the first courtyard, well placed to keep an eye on deliveries. (Alison Sim)

The Royal Household was always the biggest and best and the perquisites were so many and various that it seems amazing that any food actually reached the royal table. On the death of Queen Elizabeth her Household book was duly made up and presented to the new king, James I. In the book were included an explanation of how much everyone was paid and also the perquisites owed to them. The men who worked in the boiling house, for example, were due the dripping from roasts, the 'strippings' from the briskets, the sirloin piece of the beef and the grease left in the bottom of the pot after the beef had been boiled, whether the pot was the big lead, a kettle or a pan.[20]

These perquisites did not stop with the kitchen staff. The unbroken meats by right belonged to those who served them. These could be a great source of profit, as by no means everyone who came to Court ate at the king's expense. Many people, such as gentlemen visiting the Court on their own business, had to find their own food, so there was a good market for such ready-cooked dishes. The problem was that there was a dangerously thin line between taking what was rightfully yours and plain stealing. The Eltham Ordinances gave several stern reminders of this. Broken meats, for example (dishes which had been partly eaten), were to go to the poor, and not to be taken by members of the Household.[21]

These warnings were backed up with careful security. The clerks of the Greencloth and the clerk controller had to make daily visits to the larder and kitchens to check the stores. They also had to ensure that everyone who was expected to be there was actually at work and that nobody had either gone off on their own business or sent a deputy in to work for them. They also had to check for 'strangers' who might be hanging about trying to get free meals.

All big households had to take the same sort of care over their stores. The earl of Northumberland's accounts were also made up in great detail, so that each brew of beer or ale was carefully recorded to show how much malt was used and how much beer brewed. Sir William Petre's house steward, Edward Bell, took the same care in his accounts, and evidently economy was a consideration. During the spring of 1552 thirty-one pots of butter made at Ingatestone were sold at 5*d* each, clearly because they were surplus to requirements. This presumably would have been the valued 'May butter' described elsewhere.[22]

Everything in the Petre household, as in its royal counterpart, was carefully accounted for by tallies. These were sticks with notches cut in them to represent sums of money. The stick would then be split down the middle, and both sides involved in the transaction kept half the stick. In addition, each week Edward Bell would inspect the granaries, the millhouse, malthouse, bakehouse dairy, dovecote and storerooms. In the company of the cook he visited the larders and the other kitchen stores before checking the cellars with the butler. Every Saturday he made up his account, stating what provisions had been received that week, how much had been used and how much remained. It must have taken up a great deal of time but it was really the only way to keep pilfering in check in a large household.

Men like Edward Bell and the royal clerks of the kitchen were also responsible for provisioning their households. This was no mean feat. The Royal Household kitchens, let alone the private kitchens of the king and queen, had to produce something like six hundred covers at each meal.[23] Sir William Petre lived on a far more modest scale as he only had twenty indoor and outdoor servants at Ingatestone Hall, but the household still consumed vast quantities of food, particularly when visitors came. The hall ovens turned out some 20,000 loaves of bread in a year and even the dovecote had to provide some 1,080 birds a year.[24]

The Clerks of the Greencloth had their offices over this gateway, while at ground level the courtyard housed the boiling house and pastry. (Alison Sim)

Ingatestone was provisioned largely from produce grown on estates belonging to Sir William, but some items were bought in, such as imported wine and dried fruit. Fresh 'acates' (meat) were also bought in and there was even a part-time acater called Robert Humfrey, whose job it was to organize the provision of meat. Neither he nor Edward Bell received any wages; instead neighbouring farms were leased to them at low rents.[25]

Provisioning the Royal Household was a different matter altogether. It was not only the size of the Household that complicated matters but also the fact that the king had the ancient right known as 'prise'. This was the right to take anything he needed for his Household from his subjects at prices he set, which were, of course, somewhat short of genuine market prices. To make matters even worse, the vendor was not paid on the spot, but instead was given a receipt which he had to present to the Board of the Greencloth for payment. This might involve an expensive and troublesome journey.

In the Middle Ages the prise, though always unpopular, had worked fairly well as the Court moved a great deal and was often only in one place for a few days. By the sixteenth century, however, the system was breaking down as the Court tended to stay in the south and for longer periods in a single place, putting undue strain on certain areas. The Tudor Court was also far larger than the medieval one that the prise system had been designed to support so changes had to be made.

There were attempts to reorganize the system and even before the end of Henry VIII's reign various counties were negotiating to provide instead a given supply of certain items per year to the Court, and for a local tax to be levied to make up the shortfall. Eventually the whole system was changed so that goods were no longer supplied at all. Instead, the whole amount was met by a tax. This was simpler but no more popular.[26]

The whole system of provisioning the Court was open to considerable abuse. Before the system changed to a tax, the purveyors of various goods were given the job of providing the Court with certain items. Purveyance was not practical for highly perishable goods like milk or cream but most other staple foods were provided in this way. There were, for example, purveyors of ale, poultry, wheat and sea fish.

The purveyors had the right to make purchases at specially set reduced prices, which was why purveyance could be so profitable.

Technically speaking they were only supposed to buy what was needed for the Royal Household but obviously it was very difficult to tell if the purveyor was also buying on his own behalf. He could easily resell goods he had bought for himself at full market price and make a handsome profit.

The Eltham Ordinances show that these abuses were well known. The purveyors were warned several times both in the original Ordinances and in later additions to them not to make dishonest profit out of their position. For example, the sergeant of the bakehouse and his two purveyors were warned that wheat must be 'wholly brought to the king's garners, without converting any parte thereof to other use'.[27] The purveyors also had to present accounts at frequent intervals to the Board of the Greencloth, but this was probably not much of a check on their activities. The Court was a place where everyone was making whatever profit they could out of their own office, so it is highly unlikely that the purveyors were honest in such an atmosphere, despite the warnings.

Part of the problem of supply at this time was that transportation was so difficult. Despite the problems, though, large amounts of food did travel long distances: cattle and sheep were driven from very remote areas to the Royal Household. Other, less transportable items, were regularly shipped not only around the country but even to the Continent. The Petre's London house, used by Sir William when on royal business, was often supplied with food from Ingatestone Hall, in Essex. This journey, though, was nothing compared with the journey between Glapthorn Manor in Northamptonshire, home of the Johnson family, and the staple at Calais. The Johnsons were merchants at the staple and Sabine, John Johnson's wife, sent various foods to her husband: everything from cheeses and butter to pigeons, blackbirds and vessels of brawn.[28]

Food was considered a very acceptable gift, and gifts were very important to the Tudors. They were used as a way of reminding influential people of your existence or, of course, as bribes, but they were also used to bind families and friends together. Gifts of food could be very practical too. When William Petre's son John was christened a friend sent the Petres a guinea fowl, a mallard, a woodcock, two teals, a basket of wafers and various other cakes for the christening feast.[29] Likewise Sabine Johnson sent Margaret Baynham, a widow friend who lived in Calais, a New Year's gift of brawn and beer. The letter of thanks, which still exists, sounds a note of heartfelt gratitude, as Christmas entertaining must have been a strain on her budget.[30]

A wooden tankard taken from the wreck of the *Mary Rose*, Henry VIII's warship which sank in 1545. This was the type of drinking vessel an ordinary sailor might have owned. (Mary Rose Trust no. 83.0157)

The king himself did not feel demeaned by even very humble gifts of food. Extracts survive from Henry VII's Household book and these show that a number of small gifts of money were made to people who brought such things to the king. There is an entry 'to one that presented the king with a cake', for which the reward was 6s 8d. Another man was given 3s 4d for presenting the king with peascods. These were evidently humble people as their names are never mentioned, but even so they were not turned away.[31]

Lower down the social scale the problems of provisioning the kitchen took a different form. There is a tendency to believe that many people were self-sufficient at this time but this was by no means the case. A great number of people did grow a lot of the food they ate, but not everybody was in a position to grow everything they needed.

Independent yeomen farmers, of the type that Thomas Tusser had in mind when writing his *Five Hundred Points of Good Husbandry*, probably came closest to self-sufficiency. They had enough land to grow what they needed, but they did not mix in the social circles which required them to have large amounts of imported luxury goods. Even so, they were not self-sufficient. They still had to buy such staple items as cloth.

There were many people who were not self-sufficient simply because they did not have the opportunity to be so. If they had land, they did not have enough to support their families, and of course there were people who had no land at all. They were in a particularly vulnerable situation. If they could not find work they had no way of feeding their families.

The problem of poverty was one which grew as the sixteenth century progressed. The poor were generally better provided for in towns than in the countryside. There was a long-standing tradition of providing free or at least subsidized grain to the poorest people when times were bad. In Coventry, from 1518 to 1520, this is exactly what happened. In March 1519 a wealthy draper named John Haddon died and left £20 in his will to the Corporation to subsidize grain. The previous harvest had been poor, which must have given him the idea for the bequest. The next harvest was even worse, so the Corporation tried to control the market to keep prices down. A poor harvest the next year, too, called for stronger action, and the Corporation was forced to survey both the population and existing stocks, and then buy in almost a hundred quarters of grain to keep the poor fed.[32]

A growing population made the whole situation more difficult, so that by the end of the sixteenth century the problem of what to do about poor relief had grown a great deal worse. Larger-scale farmers were doing well while the small-scale farmer was not, which meant that the small-scale farmer often found himself forced to sell up, leaving him without land. As the problem grew, so did the cost of financing poor relief and those with means became less inclined to be charitable. The emphasis began to switch from subsidizing grain to disciplining the 'idle' unemployed.

Getting hold of the supplies needed, therefore, was not easy. Large-scale establishments had to work around the problems of how best to obtain the large quantities required without seeing excessive amounts of money or provisions disappear into other people's pockets. Small households often faced the more pressing problem of how to *afford* food rather than how to get hold of it.

CHAPTER FOUR

Beer and Brewing

When our English housewife knows how to preserve health by wholesome physic; to nourish by good meat, and to clothe the body with warm garments, she must not then by any means be ignorant in the provision of bread and drink; she must know the proportions and compositions of the same.[1]

This is how Gervase Markham begins his chapter on brewing in *The English Housewife*. Brewing was as essential a skill in a housewife as the ability to bake bread.

There was incredibly little choice of beverage in Tudor England, and almost all were alcoholic. The basic problem was that it was not a good idea to drink water. 'Water is not holesome sole by it selfe, for an Englysshe man' was how Andrew Boorde put it in *Dyetary of Health*, although his opinion was not entirely due to the quality of the water available.[2]

Sir Thomas Elyot, in his *The Castel of Helth*, does praise the drinking of water 'because it is an element, that is to say, a pure matter, where of al other lycours have their original substance but also forasmoche as it was the very naturall and fyrst drynke to all manner of creatures'.[3] He does, however, go on to comment on how careful you have to be about the source of your water.

As discussed in the previous chapter, the water supply for ordinary people was not always very reliable, whether the water was fit to drink or not. Apart from the shortages caused by illegal tapping of the water supply there were those brought on by nature. In summer, the streams and springs which fed the conduits might dry up. In winter the pipes could burst and water might simply freeze. In 1608 there were such hard frosts in King's Lynn that no water was available from the public conduit for six weeks.[4]

Milk was drunk, and is recommended by both Elyot and Boorde as especially good for the very young and very old. The problem was that for most people milk was a precious resource. Cows in the sixteenth century did not yield as much milk as they do today, and milk was needed for making cheese and butter, two essentials of everyday life. The whey left over from making cheese was all that was likely to be left for drinking for most people.

Fruit juice was not really an option for the Tudors. Unfermented grape juice, 'must', was imported but would surely have been a luxury as it cannot have lasted long. The earl of Rutland evidently had a taste, though, for it as he imported 11 gallons of Rhenish must in 1586.[5] Citrus fruits were also expensive, and even though apples and pears were widely grown, preserving the juice was impossible. The only option was to turn it into cider and perry so that the alcohol would act as a preservative. Cider and perry were still only widely drunk in certain areas of England, and like metheglin [meglithin, a kind of mead, made with honey] tended to be more of a special occasion drink. 'Certes these two [cider and perry] are very common in Sussex, Kent, Worcester, and other steads where these sorts of fruits do about, howbeit, they are not their only drink at all times but referred unto the delicate sorts of drink, as metheglin is in Wales,' is how William Harrison described their use.[6]

Tea, coffee and chocolate did not come to England until the seventeenth century and remained expensive luxuries far beyond the reach of most people for many years. It was the late eighteenth century before tea would become the ordinary person's drink in England. Their introduction revolutionized drinking and changed the way people thought about alcohol. In the sixteenth century, unless you were prepared to take a chance on drinking the water, being teetotal was simply not an option.

This did not mean that the Tudors were drunk all the time, and extremes of drunken behaviour were frowned on. William Harrison certainly had firm views on the matter and strongly denounced the behaviour of such people who 'lug at this liquor, even as pigs should lie in a row lugging at their dam's teats till they lie still again and be not able to wag'.[7] Despite the disapproval of men like Harrison, however, there does seem to have been a more relaxed attitude towards drink and drunkenness than was the case once non-alcoholic drinks became more widely available. For one thing, drinking large quantities of alcohol was simply unavoidable in certain situations.

Sir Hugh Platt, in his *Jewell House of Art and Nature* gives instructions on 'how to prevent drunkenesse'. He excuses himself for providing the information, saying that he intends it 'onely for the helpe of such modest drinkers as sometimes in companie are drawne, or rather forced to pledge in full bolles such quaffing companions as they would be loth of offend'.[8] Drinking was a vital part of social events, and drinking various toasts to members of the company was seen as polite – to refuse was unthinkably bad manners. A toast did not consist of a polite sip from your glass, as it would do today. It consisted of draining your glass completely.[9] An evening in the company of those you did not wish, or could not afford, to offend was bound to be a drunken one, and getting drunk was certain to be a fairly regular event for anyone, however modest a drinker they wished to be. Incidentally, Sir Hugh's advice was not much use anyway. He suggests either the age-old standby of drinking milk before you go out, or else drinking a large draft of salad oil. Presumably the salad oil was supposed to make you feel too sick to want to drink.

The main beverages available to the Tudors were ale, beer, or wine. Wine was an expensive import, and so was really only available regularly to the middle and upper classes. Most people drank ale or beer, which was why brewing was such an essential skill. Beer and ale was so widely drunk that many foreigners commented on it and considered it the national drink. 'The general drink is ale, which is prepared from barley, and is excellently well tasted, but strong and intoxicating,' commented Paul Hentzner, a visiting jurist from Brandenburg.[10]

The process of brewing beer was basically the same as it is today, though of course without all the elaborate technology which now controls the process so carefully. The first step was malting the grain, which was usually barley. Grain contains a store of food in the form of starch and protein, but the brewer needs to turn this to sugar, as it is sugar which will eventually turn into alcohol. Grain contains enzymes that turn the starch and protein to sugar, but to do this the barley has to be germinated. This was done by steeping the grain in water. The germination process must not be allowed to carry on for too long, though, so at just the right stage the grain has to be dried in a kiln to stop further growth.

Markham goes into great detail about making malt[11] but in practice many households bought the malt in. Malting was a process which required the right weather. If you tried to make

The processes involved in making beer. In the background the wort is being heated. In the foreground on the right it is being cooled and on the left it is being poured into barrels. (Samantha Doty)

malt in hot weather the grain would often sprout too much, and in cold weather it was hard to get it to sprout at all. The malting process required careful supervision and it must have been quite a problem for a housewife to cope with it on top of all her other work. The space to make the malt must have been lacking too if you lived in a town, as one stage of the process requires it to be laid on the floor in a thin layer. In any case, it was easy enough to buy, though this did not eliminate the hard work. For the best results you had to grind the malt just before you used it, so even if you bought your malt you still had to put it through the mill before you could brew.

The next stage was mashing. This process continues the conversion of the starch and protein to sugar. The dried malt is ground up then mixed with hot water. After a time the liquid, which is now called wort by brewers, was drawn off. The malt, once used to its full extent, was then fed to the pigs, as Thomas Tusser reminds us in his usual dreadful verse:

> In buing of drink by the firkin or pot
> the tallie ariseth, but hog amendes not.[12]

Selective breeding has made farm animals very different from the ones known to the Tudors. This is a Tamworth pig, believed to be similar to those familiar in the sixteenth century. (Weald and Downland Open Air Museum/Alison Sim)

He was reminding the housewife that if she bought in beer or ale, not only would it cost more but her pig would not grow fat.

The next stage was boiling. The wort was boiled up with hops for between one and two hours. After this, the spent hops were strained out of the wort, and the mixture was cooled in shallow wooden trays or tubs. This was followed by fermentation, when the cooled wort was put into a barrel to ferment, and yeast was added. The yeast fed off the sugar and produced alcohol and carbon dioxide. The surplus yeast collected as a froth on top of the liquid. This was very important, as it provided yeast for bread making, which is why bread ovens and brewhouses are often found together in old houses. The final stage of the process was called racking. Once fermentation was complete, the beer would be run off from the yeast debris into casks, where it would be kept until it was needed.

The key stage in this process was the addition of hops. Today these are so much part of the brewing of beer that you might think they have always grown in England, but if fact they were only introduced from Flanders in the late fifteenth century. Before that time ale was the usual drink in England. This was very similar to beer but without the hops.

The study of brewing is made all the more confusing by the use of a number of different terms. For example, some brewers[13] in the sixteenth century were referring to the stronger beers as 'ales' even if they were brewed with hops. However, to make matters easier, here the term 'beer' is used to mean a drink flavoured with hops.

The change over to brewing with hops was certainly not welcomed by everyone. 'Ale for an Englysshe man is a naturall drynke,' declared Andrew Boorde, whereas beer was 'a naturall drynke for a Dutche man'. Boorde sees this new-fangled drink as bad for the nation's health: 'And nowe of late dayes it is moche used in Englande to the detryment of many Englysshe men, specyally it kylleth them the which be troubled with the colycke, and the stone and the strangulation, for the drykne is a cole drynke, yet it doth make a man fat and doth inflate the bely, as it doth appere by the Dutche mens faces and belyes.'[14] Nobody took any notice of these dire warnings, which was just as well, as the health of the nation did not seem to suffer as a result of this development.

The change in the south of England at least seems to have been complete by the end of the sixteenth century. John Stow comments that in 1563 heavy rain ruined the hop crop in Zealand, and hops became so expensive in London that some brewers resorted to using broom and bay berries instead. Brewing with hops had obviously become the norm.[15] In the north the change took longer. The climate was too cold to grow hops there, which made them both harder to obtain and more expensive than in the south.

Sir Hugh Platt was so concerned about the shortage of hops that he recommended the use of wormwood instead. Wormwood was usually seen as a medicinal plant and Sir Hugh went to great lengths to explain that in a weaker form the herb is quite safe to use in everyday drink. Whatever his opinions, however, wormwood never came close to replacing hops.[16]

The change was gradual, but it was far-reaching. The use of hops made beer a very different drink from the ale it replaced. Hops acted as a preservative, so while most ales had not lasted long, beer could keep for months. The best quality beers, 'March' or 'October' beers as they were known, could keep for much longer. William Harrison comments:

Beer that is used at noblemen's tables in their fixed and standing houses is commonly of a year old or peradventure of two years' tunning or more, but this is not general. It is also brewed in March and therefore called March beer, but for the household it is usually not under a month's age, each one coveting to have the same stale as he may, so that it be not sour . . .'[17]

Tin glazed earthenware
tankard, mounted in silver.
This is a 'Malling jug' which
would have been imported
from Germany and is the type
of drinking vessel described by
Etienne Perlin. It is now in the
British Museum. (Julie Anne
Hudson)

'Sour' in this context does not mean off, but aged. Strong March beer
improved with age, so it was no wonder everyone wanted older beer.
There were ways of 'maturing' it quickly: Sir Hugh Platt suggests
burying bottled beer for forty-eight hours.[18]

Ale would go off very quickly, particularly in hot weather, so that it
would tend to be brewed in small quantities for more or less
immediate use. Beer must have been far more convenient for women,
as they had to brew far less often. William Harrison comments that his
wife and her maid-servants brewed, using hops, only once a month.[19]

It was not all good news, though. Beer needed to be boiled for longer than ale, and it also required specialist equipment. For one thing, it was advisable to have a separate brewhouse with a special furnace (a fire enclosed in brick) on which to boil the liquid. If you boiled the beer over the fire in the kitchen it was all too easy to tip scalding-hot liquid all over yourself, or to set the house alight if the fire got out of control. One blaze which left a third of the population of the Cheshire town of Nantwich homeless in December 1583 started in exactly this way.[20]

The fact that beer would keep longer meant that it could be brewed in large quantities, making a proper brewhouse necessary. Even quite small households had a brewhouse. There has been no proper study of small-scale brewhouses, but in Steyning in Sussex by the 1660s it seems that a third of households had one, including those belonging to small farmers and skilled manual workers.[21]

The fact that hopped beer kept better than ale revolutionized brewing, as it allowed beer to be brewed on a large scale as a business. As ale did not keep, it was not really practical to brew on a large scale, so you brewed ale as you needed it, just as you baked your bread. Brewing was very much a woman's job, and selling ale was usually a sideline, something that many women seem to have done only when they needed some extra money, and it was just a case of making a little extra ale to sell when doing the family brew.

Licences to brew ale for sale were usually granted to women who were not able to maintain themselves in other ways, such as poor widows. Many alehouses were very small, no more than a room in someone's house.[22] Alehouses were definitely distrusted by the authorities as they were seen as places where the poor could get up to no good. John Skelton, in his poem 'The tunnyng of Elynour Rummynge', caricatures the alewife of the time:

> Her lothely lere
> Is nothynge clere
> But ugly of chere
> Dropsy and drowsy
> Scurvey and lowsy
> Her face allbowsy
> Comely crynklyd
> Woundersly wrynkled
> Lyke a rost pygges erer
> Brystled wyth here.[23]

Elynour's brew is as disgusting as her appearance, as she allows her hens to roost in the alehouse and their dung gets into the ale. Her alehouse is also a resort for the local prostitutes. How accurate Skelton's picture is in describing a typical alehouse is not known, but certainly they were only for the poor. The upper and middle classes went to taverns and inns, which were far more luxurious and provided both a grander setting and fine food and drink. The fact that 'respectable' people never went to alehouses was another reason for the middle and upper classes to distrust them.

Beer brewing soon became more than just a convenient sideline, and William Harrison even talks of beer being exported.[24] As it was a far more stable drink than ale it could withstand the vigours of being transported. Ale brewing had been part of domestic life, but large-scale beer brewing took place outside the home, and women gradually began to be excluded from it. This is not to say that all home brewing suddenly stopped, but certainly the rise of the large-scale brewer pushed women out of brewing on an industrial scale.

Certainly there was great demand for beer. Households consumed quantities which would surprise us today. It is important to be aware though, when looking at household accounts, that the rations of food listed are not always for one person alone. It was usual to serve food in messes (portions) of four, so that the portions mentioned in accounts may have served four people rather than one. The earl of Northumberland's household accounts are a good example. They show that either a potell (4 pints) or a gallon (8 pints) of beer tended to be served with each portion of food. Both amounts are easily divisible by four, so that each person may have been given either one or two pints of beer with his meal. This seems much more likely than each person receiving the whole amount on their own. The lord and lady of the house had 1 quart (2 pints) of beer and another of wine between them at most meals, which would be 2 pints of liquid each. If other households had to provide 2 pints of beer for every adult at each meal you could imagine how much beer even a small household would get through.[25]

Brewing was very skilled work. Temperature control is very important in all the processes, but thermometers were not available to brewers in the sixteenth century and they had to learn to judge by experience how things were progressing. It was also far harder to control equipment in the brewhouse than it is today. The copper, the large vessel used for boiling (which incidentally might not be made of copper at all, but of lead),[26] required particularly careful handling.

Salt glazed stoneware bottle with three medallions moulded with a crowned Tudor rose and Elizabeth I's royal cypher. It was made at Frechen, near Cologne, 1590–1600. These items were made for the export trade, hence the decoration. (Julie Anne Hudson)

Once the wort was drained out of it, the copper would start to burn after only a few minutes unless it was either refilled or the fire underneath it extinguished and the hot coals raked away.

The end of the brewhouse where cooling and fermentation took place had to be kept cool, which meant having unglazed windows, usually fitted with louvres. Brewhouses were draughty places, so it must have been hard providing the correct conditions for the yeast. We know today that yeast needs a working temperature of between

60 and 70 degrees, which must have been very difficult to maintain when, under the same roof, the wort was being boiled and the finished product cooled.[27] The problem of controlling the temperature also made it very difficult to brew in hot weather, which was why the best beer was brewed in March or October, when it was neither too hot nor too cold.

Brewing was also very hard work. It involved moving around large amounts of liquid, some of which was hot and difficult to handle. Pumps were gradually introduced into brewhouses but it is unlikely that there were very many in use in the sixteenth century. Long hours were also the norm, as the processes could not be switched on or off to fit around the working day. The timetable recommended in the brewhouse at Woburn in 1837 gives an indication of how it must have been even in the sixteenth century. The first mash was at 5 a.m., although filling and heating the copper might have taken between one and two hours, which could have meant a 3 a.m. start. The beer would have been ready for the fermenting tun in the early evening, so that the yeast could be added before the brewers finished for the night.[28] Brewing was not for the faint hearted.

The taste and strength of the resulting brew would have varied a great deal. Just as today, beers were deliberately brewed to different tastes and strengths. The malt would be used several times when brewing beer. The first use of the malt was for the best and strongest beer. The second would produce a weaker beer, and the third, 'small' beer.

Producing small beer was seen as a bonus by brewers as basically it paid for the fuel used for making the whole brew. By the time the malt was used for the third time it would be producing beer that was unpleasantly bitter and very weak. This was the brew that was commonly given to servants. Other, stronger beer was often kept in a locked cellar, but generally there was free access to the small beer as it was a drink cheap enough to allow anyone to drink whenever they were thirsty. In any case, it was so weak that it did not keep and needed to be consumed.

Beer was sometimes specifically brewed to be fairly weak, however. It was only the stronger March or October beer which kept all year. Other beer lasted a few months, but no longer. This meant that some brewing had to go on in the summer, when conditions were difficult. There was also more demand for weaker beer at this time of year, as during the hot summer months large quantities of refreshing, low-alcohol drink would be needed. Busy times of the year like haymaking must have kept the brewers hard at work. Fortunately the low specific gravity of the weaker beer meant that it was possible to brew it in warm weather, though the work must have been very unpleasant for the brewer.

'Ordinary' beer of the type that Gervase Markham mentions would probably have been of about the same strength as the type of beer that we would expect to drink in a pub today. March or October beer was much stronger, and was probably what Paul Hentzner was served (see p. 47). The taste of the beer would have varied according to the brewer, as there were many ways of changing it. For example, Markham suggests adding oak boughs and a pewter dish to the wort to give 'bite' to the brew.[29]

Moving beer around was not an easy task. It had to be kept in wooden barrels, which had a tendency to leak. The 'brewer's dozen' might contain anything between thirteen and fifteen barrels, to compensate for the amount of beer that could leak or spoil in transit.[30] Beer tuns were not cheap to transport. For example, the earl of Northumberland paid 2*s* for the hire of three carts to transport 3 tuns of beer (a tun contained 252 gallons) between his two properties of Wresill and Topcliff.[31] The Johnson family, who were well-to-do merchants, sent a present of a barrel of beer to a friend at Christmas one year. It cost 4*s* 10*d* to send from the family's home at Glapthorne, Northamptonshire, to the friend's home in Calais, which was quite a lot of money.[32] It was no wonder that every town had its own brewery and that so many people brewed at home.

The weaker types of beer did not keep indefinitely and so they did have to be fairly carefully looked after. Several household books gave instructions on how to revive beer that was beginning to turn sour. Sir Hugh Platt, for example, recommends putting a handful or two of ground malt into the beer barrel which should then be well stirred. He also suggests burying sour beer for twenty-four hours or adding new, strong beer; alternatively oyster shells or salt.[33] It was very likely that a housewife just had to reconcile herself to throwing away sour beer, especially in summer.

Beer in the sixteenth century was a great deal more than just a drink. It was a vital part of the diet. Most people consider the sixteenth century to have been a prosperous time for England, but this was only the case for the middle and upper classes. Real wages for ordinary people were falling. The price of barley in 1600 was about six times what it had been in 1500,[34] so that the introduction of beer to replace ale was important. The malt could be used several times when brewing beer, which made it cheaper. In Boston in 1547 best ale retailed at around a penny-three-farthings a gallon whereas best beer was a penny-ha'penny.[35]

Beer was not only drunk cold. It was frequently heated up, and for special occasions might be spiced and all sorts of things added. Roasted apples, eggs and toast were among the ingredients frequently added to celebration drinks. 'Lambswool', a beverage made of roasted apples, beer, nutmegs, ginger and sugar, was regularly drunk at Christmas. It took its name from the froth which floated on the surface.

Beer was regarded primarily not as a drink but as a food. Three pints a day would have given a young boy a quarter of the calories he required. Beer would also have provided all the main nutrients, except fat, which people needed. It was also an important source of vitamin B. The price of beer also went up more slowly than the price of food so for ordinary people it really was a vital part of their diet. It was not just a drink, it was an essential part of everyday life.

CHAPTER FIVE

Wine

'But to saye as I thynke, I suppose, neither ale nor biere is to be compared to wyne . . .'[1] This was the opinion expressed by Sir Thomas Elyot in his manual *The Castel of Helth* and he echoed the views of all wealthy Tudors. Beer was all very well when you were thirsty, but that was as far as it went. Wine was the drink for a gentleman as it was a sign that you could afford the finer things in life. It was, quite simply, *the* drink to offer your guests, and to be seen drinking yourself.

The basic reason for this was that wine had to be imported and was therefore expensive. Frederick, Duke of Wurtemburg, who visited England in the reign of Elizabeth I, remarked that 'there is no wine-growing in this kingdom; but if you want wine you can purchase the best and most delicious sorts, of various varieties, and that on account of the great facility which the sea affords them for barter with other countries.'[2] Vines had been grown in England in the twelfth and thirteenth centuries but by the sixteenth century the practice had died out. Climatic changes may have been to blame, as Soranzo, the Venetian envoy in London, indicates: 'Although they have vines they do not make wine of any sort, the plant serving as an ornament for their gardens, rather than anything else, as the grapes do not ripen save in very small quantities, partly because the sun has not much power, and partly because precisely at the ripening season cold winds generally prevail, so that the grapes wither . . .'[3] This observation is borne out by other evidence. Thomas Hill's *Gardener's Labyrinth*, first published in 1577, does give information on how to grow vines but the emphasis is on growing them to cover arbours to provide shade in the summer months.[4]

As Duke Frederick points out, the variety of imports made up for the lack of home-grown wine, though they could only be had for a price. Anything which had to be imported was expensive. To the better-off, this was part of the charm of wine. It was valued not only for its flavour, but also for its cost. In an age when status symbols were important, it was the drink that anyone who was anyone drank. According to the household accounts of the Earl of Northumberland, it was only the earl and his lady who regularly drank wine and the cellar was required to be closely monitored: 'Item: that the said Clerkis of the Brevements[5] allow no wyne for Drynkyngs of the Yeoman or Grome of the Sellar except it be by recorde of an Usher Nor Wyne to be allowid that is served for Meales in the Great Chambre or in the Hall except it be by record of an Usher of the Chambre or of the hal and they to be at the Brevement.'[6]

Even in wine-producing countries poorer people needed to sell their wine and could not afford to drink it themselves. They made do with 'piquette', made by adding water to the waste wine skins.[7]

It is noteworthy that Thomas Tusser makes no mention at all of wine in his *Five Hundred Points of Good Husbandry*, even though he gives information on everything from brewing to how to deal with vermin. His book was aimed at more ordinary folk than most of the other household manuals. If his audience bought wine they would do so in small quantities to consume immediately. It was only the well-to-do who could buy wine in large quantities and who needed instructions on how to look after it.

The cost of wine could be very high indeed. For one thing, the handling charges involved in transporting bulky wine tuns across the sea and then into England were considerable. In 1528 Roger Basyng brought Bordeaux wine for Henry VIII: 152 tuns of a mixture of red, white and claret wines. The lighterage to take the wine from Blackwall to the crane in the vintry where it could be unloaded cost 4*d* a tun, the cranage 2*d* a tun and winding and rolling cost 4*d* a tun. The total cost of bringing the whole shipment from France, including other fees such as cooperage (the cost of the barrels etc.), came to £844 12*s* 4*d*, or £5 16*s* 4*d* a ton. Compared with the average wage of a labourer, about £2 a year, this was quite a sum.[8]

The wine itself was an expensive commodity too, although then, as now, its price varied considerably depending on quality and availability. In 1488 Oriel College, Cambridge, bought red, white and claret wine for 8*d* a gallon, but in 1523 in the same town a rundlet (18 gallons) of malmsey, a much better quality wine, cost 1*s* a gallon. The sum of 8*d* a gallon seems to have been a standard wholesale price for several years, but wine was just like any other agricultural crop. A bad harvest meant the price would rise. In 1587

The 'Agas' map of Elizabethan London. Cranes for unloading ships can be seen working in the place marked 'Three Crans'. It was for the use of cranes like these that 'cranage' had to be paid when importing wine. (Guildhall Library, Corporation of London)

a gallon of claret bought in Norwich cost *2s 4d*. This was due not only to a gradual rise in the price of wine throughout the century but also to bad harvests causing a shortage.[9]

Most of the wine industry was very tightly controlled. It was of enormous political significance as it was a great source of income to the Crown. There were heavy import duties to be paid, by both native and foreign merchants. The granting of licences to import given quantities of wine free of duty was also a useful and fairly cheap way for the Crown to reward its supporters. The wine fleet often found itself caught up in political disagreements between monarchs. In 1521, when relations between France and England took a turn for the worse, some of the ships of the fleet that went to Bordeaux were confiscated by the French.[10]

Before wine could be put on sale in England it had to be gauged. This was a way of checking the quantity of wine in a cask, as the cask might not necessarily be full. Markham gives a list of gauge marks so that the housewife can be sure of how much wine she is buying. The mark would verify the amount said to be in the cask.[11] The wine was not allowed to be sold until the gauger, the royal officer responsible for checking the wine, had put his mark on the cask to show that it had been tested and the import duties paid. However, the wine was still monitored after this stage. There were searchers whose job it was to find and dispose of unfit wine. Unfit wine seems to have been quite a problem: in 1528 in the east of the city, the London searchers found 21 tuns and 2 hogsheads (a hogshead contained 63 gallons) of red, claret and white wine and 42 tuns and 1 butt (a butt contained 126 gallons) of various sweet wines. In the west of the city the total was even higher: 41 tuns and 1 hogshead of red, claret and white wine and 71 tuns of sweet wines.[12]

It is not surprising that the searchers found so much unfit wine. We tend to see wine as something which has hardly changed over the centuries but this is not the case. Modern wine production, like modern brewing, involves the use of a great deal of sophisticated technology. Sixteenth-century wine was a much less stable product than its modern counterpart and could go off very easily. Most wine producers aimed to get the new vintage off their hands as soon as possible for this very reason. In his treatise on wine and cider written in the sixteenth century Julien de Paulmier comments that most of the wines of France and Germany are at their best after a year, but that in a cold, damp year the wines turn sour within twelve months. As a rule, he says, most wines have reached their perfect state within three or four months of the vintage and will not last more than a year. It was only the stronger wines from further south which lasted longer.[13]

Wine was also a very difficult substance to transport and store, especially as it had to be kept and transported in wooden barrels. It was not that nobody had thought of using glass bottles. In a letter dated 24 August 1538, Sir William Penison, writing to Cromwell, commented that he 'had provided for Lady Motrell white and claret wine, during the time of her abiding, at dinners and suppers in flagons, as if it were sent in hogsheads it would be unfined and unmete to drink so soone'.[14] The problem was that glass bottles could not be produced on a large scale cheaply enough to allow all wine to be stored in them. Instead, wine had to be kept in barrels, which not only leaked, they also tended to let air in.

The result was that by the time the new vintage came around most of the previous year's wine would be past drinking, so that there was a race to import the new wine in time for Christmas. This was more of a struggle than you might think. Buying the wine and loading it on to the ships took time and the sea journey from Bordeaux to an English port could take weeks rather than the few days it would take today. In 1597 the Bordeaux fleet only returned to London on 12 December and the next year they were expected to arrive on the 18th.[15]

Despite the short lifespan of wine, it was not a good idea to drink it too young. Very new wine would upset your stomach. Henry VIII took advantage of this as yet another way of making life unpleasant for Katherine of Aragon, once he had discarded her. In 1534 Katherine sent to Chapuys, the ambassador of the Holy Roman Emperor and a personal friend and supporter, asking for some old Spanish wine. Henry would only allow her new wine, and as her health was failing by this time it was the last thing she needed. She was given the old wine, but the servant who organized the gift was dismissed for obeying her order, as it was contrary to the king's wishes.[16]

Sixteenth-century wine also differed from modern wine in that the mixture of grape varieties that went into it was not always strictly controlled. Several different varieties of grape would be planted in one vineyard to minimize the risks for the farmer. The different varieties would ripen at different times, so that there was less chance of the entire crop being ruined by adverse weather. It was quite a sensible arrangement in that the riper grapes would add sugar to the wine while others would add acidity, but it made the end result rather unpredictable.[17]

Making wine in the sixteenth century. A wine press can be seen in the background. (Samantha Doty)

The grapes would be trodden in a trough or shallow vat. Red wine had to be put into a deep vat in which the juice and skin could ferment together, to allow the colour from the skins to leach into the wine. The obvious short cut was to tread grapes for red wine in the deep vat in which they would be fermented, but this was dangerous. As the grapes fermented they gave off carbon dioxide, and this could not easily escape from a deep vat. Consequently the grape treaders could be suffocated.[18]

Wine presses were also used, but only to extract 15 to 20 per cent of the juice from white grapes, or to extract wine from the red grapes after they had been fermented. The *vin de presse* was inferior to the *vin de goutte*, which was run off from the vats after the treaders had been at work. The *vin de presse* contained extra tannin and colour in the case of red wine, but tannin only really became desirable once wine began to be kept for longer. In wine that is to be drunk very young tannin just gives an unpleasantly bitter taste.

Keeping wine was very difficult even for the owners of the vineyards, before all the problems of transportation had been solved. The use of sulphur, a practice which is still used today, was first documented in 1487.[19] Sulphur kills microbes and protects wine from the effects of oxygen, preventing spoilage and browning. It was added by burning wood shavings which had been soaked in powdered sulphur, herbs and incense in the casks before they were filled. This did not mean that keeping wine ceased to be a problem, however, and housewifery manuals and manuals on wine go into great detail on keeping wine, and how to counteract the effects of it spoiling.

Arnald of Villanova wrote a book on wine in the thirteenth century. It continued to be read for centuries, though, and was the first book on the subject ever to be printed. Reading it, it soon becomes clear just how difficult it was looking after wine. Villanova emphasizes the need for clean casks which have been well washed with saltwater and then fumigated with incense and myrrh. He suggests putting chips of juniper wood into fermenting wine, or suspending a linen bag containing the flowers of hops or seeds of rye into wine once it has fermented. Another problem was how to judge exactly what state a wine was in. If wine was beginning to go off, it was essential to find this out before it was so far gone that nothing could be done to redeem it. Villanova suggests putting suspect wine into a new cask, and sealing some of the lees left behind in a small jar. If the lees smell bad after three days, the wine will spoil.[20]

The weather was another factor to contend with. Certain types of conditions were particularly dangerous for wine, such as when it was humid and thundery. Dough made from rye, wrapped in a linen cloth and put into the bung-hole of the cask was recommended to protect wines from the effects of this.[21] Extremes of temperature were a problem too. Villanova advises that wine cellars must be heated and have small windows which can be opened or closed according to the temperature. Heating a wine cellar must have been quite an undertaking at a time when a fire was a luxury in some households.

As wine was so expensive nobody wanted to throw it out. Housewives were inundated with advice on how to revive wine that was no longer at its best. Sir Hugh Platt suggests putting a piece of cheese in the cast with 'a wine that reboyleth' in the hot summer months.[22] Markham devotes pages of *The English Housewife* to keeping, restoring and serving wine. For example, white wine that had lost its colour could be restored by adding 3 gallons of new milk which had had the cream removed. This was then beaten into the wine. Markham also suggests adding alum to the wine, which might help, at least temporarily, in the case of wine which had spoiled because of bacteria.[23]

However, it was not only housewives who were keen to make their wines appear better than they were. The vintners had a professional interest in doing so. Vintners seem to have been regarded rather in the way that modern society views used-car salesmen. There were honest vintners but you had to be careful. Advice is given on this theme by Rustican, who wrote about wine in the fourteenth century; as with Villanova's book, it was still read for a long time afterwards and was translated into French at the orders of Charles V in 1486. In it he recommends tasting wine when *'le vent de midy'* was blowing. Villanova explains this idea more fully: 'It is also good that the wine be tasted when the wind called Auster, which comes from midday, blows, for at that time which is in autumn, wines are changed more easily and reveal whatever weakness they might have.'[24]

Villanova and Rustican also agree that wine should not be tasted on either a full or an empty stomach, or after eating anything bitter or salty.[25] They both warn against unscrupulous wine merchants who offer inexperienced wine tasters cheese or salty nuts before tasting wine, thus ruining their palates. There were other tricks a wine merchant could get up to. A favourite was to give a customer one wine to taste, but to sell him a totally different one. This was why a wine merchant's cellar door had always to be left open during hours of business so that everyone could see what he was up to. Sir Hugh Platt, too, reveals some of the vintner's more dishonest tricks. Sack, a Portuguese wine and forerunner of sherry, could be made to look whiter by adding lime. Honey and cloves could make a wine sweeter, cloudy wines could be made clear by adding eggs, milk bay salt and conduit water, beaten together. If wine was beginning to go off, the vintner could add turnsole (a plant used to make a deep red or violet dye), starch or 'manie other Drugges, and aromaticall ware which he fetcheth from the Apothecarie'.[26] Sir Hugh was so incensed by the underhand dealings of the vintners that he even makes a threat: 'But my purpose is onely to put some in minde of these grosse night-woorkes which discover themselves by candlelight at their Celler Windowes, wishing them to leave all unwholesome practizes for mans bodies least if they should hereafter against my will force mee to publish them to the worlde . . .'

Example of glass made in England, now in the British Museum. The date 1586 appears on the other side. The inscription reads 'In God is all my Trust'. (Copyright British Museum)

In fairness to the vintners, it must be stated that they were put under considerable pressure. There was a set price or 'assize' for wine, and often there was very little room for a reasonable profit margin. This obviously encouraged fraudulent practices as they simply would not have been able to afford to waste much of the wine. There still seems to have been enough money in the wine trade to make it an attractive proposition, though. Many people who were not members of the Vintners' Company were licensed to sell wine as a sideline and there were plenty of people who were willing to risk selling without a licence. In December 1568 Roger Richardson, merchant taylor, William Hamsworth, clothworker, and Thomas Parkyns, cooper, were all accused of this.

The problems involved in buying and storing wine and the dishonesty of the vintners did not diminish people's taste for it, and the wide variety available increased in the sixteenth century. Members of the expanding middle classes wanted wine as well as all the other comforts that they could now afford. Sir Hugh Platt complains about how fussy the English had become about wine, suggesting that the vintners could not be held entirely to blame for doctoring wines 'for we are growne so nice in taste that almost no winis unlesse they be more pleasant that they can bee of the Group will content us, nay no colour unlesse it be perfect, fine and bright, will satisfie our wanton eyes'.[27]

The long association of England with Gascony had made claret, the wine produced there, a favourite since the Middle Ages. It was very much wine for everyday drinking, though. The stronger, sweeter wines were more highly valued. There had been a general taste for sweet things since the Middle Ages, so this was not surprising. There was also a practical reason for valuing sweet wines. They might contain as much as 17 degrees of alcohol, which meant that they were much easier to handle than the weaker wines from places like Gascony. The higher level of alcohol meant that they kept better and withstood long journeys well. They could even mature in the cask and they certainly kept far longer than the weaker wines. Julien de Paulmier comments that they might keep five or six years, or even longer.[28]

At the time of the crusades the sweet wines coming to England had been grown in the Levant, that is, Syria, Lebanon and Palestine. Much of the wine was also grown on Candia (Crete). The term used generally to describe these wines was malmsey, or malvasia, a corruption of the name of the town of Monemvasia, which was a large supplier of wine. In the sixteenth century the sweet wines came from the Mediterranean, especially from Cyprus. In the hot sun the grapes reached a very high sugar content which was further boosted by late harvesting and by half drying the grapes before they were trodden. The methods used by the Cypriots were described by Estienne de Lusignan in 1572. He observed that the grapes were ripe at the end of July, but were not picked until September. They were then dried for three days on the roofs of the houses.[29] Once the grapes had been trodden the juice would be put into jars. These jars would then be buried to control the rate of fermentation so that as much of the sugar as possible would turn into alcohol. Even so, there was often sugar left in the wine, so that it would have been pleasantly sweet but also strong. Before distilled spirits became common, such sweet wines would have been the strongest drink available. They were very expensive, usually costing twice as much as claret. In 1500 Gascony wine was selling at 8*d* a gallon in Cambridge, while sweet wine cost 1*s* 4*d* a gallon.[30]

The English love of sweet wines gave parliament and the Crown an excellent chance to raise revenue. The subsidy, a tax on wine which was granted to the Crown by parliament and which was quite separate from the import duty, was always considerably higher on sweet wines. When the subsidy on French or Rhenish wine was 2*s* or 3*s* a tun, the subsidy on sweet wines might be 4*s* or even 6*s* a tun.[31]

Increasing amounts of wine were also being imported from Spain, and then, when relations with Spain deteriorated, from Portugal. There was certainly no lack of wine for those who could afford it.

Like beer, wine was drunk not only as it came but was often flavoured. Hippocras, or spiced wine, had been drunk since the Middle Ages. It could be a luxurious drink, as the spices were not cheap. It could also be used as a good way of using up wine that was going off, as the spices would mask the flavour. Markham suggests adding ginger, cloves, nutmeg and a large quantity of sugar (4 lb to make a gallon of wine), showing what a very sweet tooth the English had at the time.[32] Wine could also be served warm, just as beer was. In the absence of non-alcoholic hot beverages, warm beer and wine would have been the only hot drinks available.

Distilled wine, or *aqua vitae*, was also becoming known in the sixteenth century, though it was seen more as a medicine than anything else. In 1525 a translation of Jerome Braunscheweig's *The Vertuose Boke of Distyllacyoun* was published in England, 'for the help and profit of surgeons, physicians, pothecaries and all manner of people', though it was not aimed at vintners. Various herbs were commonly distilled at this time as a way of preserving them for the winter.

The claims made for distilled spirits were extraordinary. They were supposed to do everything from helping sore eyes to preserving youth, and were taken like medicine, in small quantities of about five or six drops. By the mid-sixteenth century the English were obviously beginning to see these spirits as more than medicine. In 1559, when Peter Morwyng published his *Treasure of Eronymous*, there were already a number of professional distillers in London. They made alcohol from wine lees and unsound wine which they bought from the vintners. This is why Sir Hugh Platt complains about the vintners adulterating wine which was really only fit to be sold to the *aqua vitae* men.[33] As there was already a tavern called Le Aqua Vitae Howse in London by 1572 it seems unlikely that these professional distillers were only catering for medicinal needs.[34]

The English love of wine in the sixteenth century was such that even William Harrison, writing at a time when fierce patriotism was the rule, and after praising the fertility of England and the fine quality of its agricultural products, was forced to admit that there was 'one benefit which our nation wanteth, and that is wine'.[35] At least Harrison could comfort himself with the certainty that he had enough money to indulge in the luxury of drinking it.

CHAPTER SIX

Health and Diet

For a number of reasons it is difficult to decide just how healthy the Tudor diet was. One is that even today nobody is sure exactly what the human body needs in terms of nutrition. Humans survive and have survived in the past on a huge range of diets, from completely vegetarian to living entirely on meat and animal products. Nutritional needs also vary with age, sex, levels of activity and even the air temperature. Because of the number of variants involved, it is only possible to speak in general terms.

It is also difficult to know exactly what the effects of bad diet are. Modern studies of malnutrition are usually carried out on sections of the population living in poverty. This means that the health problems found among the group may be due as much to poor living conditions or ignorance of how to avoid health risks as to bad diet.

It is important not to assume that malnourishment was at the root of all Tudor health problems. There used to be a general belief that widescale malnourishment weakened the population, allowing infectious diseases like the plague to take hold. There are indeed certain diseases, such as tuberculosis, which are more likely to occur in a malnourished person, but this is not always the case. For example, the plague and the various forms of influenza were among the great killer diseases of the sixteenth century. If it were true that malnutrition increased susceptibility to them, you might expect that a poor harvest would be followed by an outbreak of one of these diseases, but this was not so. Periods of food shortage in the 1550s and late 1590s did not trigger outbreaks of either disease. Epidemics often occurred when food was not in short supply at all.[1] Another, more recent, example is the great 'flu epidemic which followed the First World War. For years it was generally assumed that malnutrition during the war had weakened the population. It is now believed that malnutrition had very little to do with it.[2] The issue is further complicated by the fact that some illnesses can stop the body absorbing essential nutrients, thereby aggravating malnutrition: for example, the various diseases which have diarrhoea as a symptom.

If the problems involved in studying our own nutrition are complex, those of trying to study the effects of nutrition in the past are even more so. Firstly, there is the difficulty of knowing precisely what people ate. We are not exactly sure what the bulk of the population in Tudor times was eating. Even modern studies rarely examine what individual subjects are eating, but generalize and make assumptions based on body weight, the amount of fat that most people are carrying and so on.

We know in general terms that the Tudors ate bread and pottage and that they drank ale or beer, but we do not know, for example, how much fresh fruit they ate (when it was available). The exact quantity of fresh vegetables eaten even by the rich is also a mystery. Both factors are important when considering how healthy a diet is. The other problem is the lack of written information. Parish registers, which are the best sources of information about deaths at a local level, are often incomplete. If they do survive, often they do not give the cause of death, and even when the cause of death is given it is impossible to say for sure whether malnutrition was anything to do with it or not. It is understandable that this whole area is still very much a matter for debate even among historians.

A good place to start is to consider what conditions were probably like in the sixteenth century. Generally health seems to have been better than is often assumed. Take child mortality rates. By modern standards the figures are horrific, but they are not as high as they are often thought to be. The frequently made assumption that half of all babies born did not live to the age of ten seems to be an exaggeration. The figure is probably closer to a quarter at the most.[3]

Fortunately the chances of dying of starvation in England were also very low. Historians disagree about exactly how low but the only possible case of actual famine in the sixteenth century occurred in the counties of Westmorland and Cumberland in 1587–8 and 1597. These counties were particularly remote and poor communications made it difficult to import food. Conditions there were not typical of England as a whole.[4] However, the fear of starvation was very real indeed, and it is the fear rather than the reality which tends to be remembered.

Parish registers show that those who did die of starvation often were wandering beggars. They were an especially vulnerable group, but fortunately even at the end of the sixteenth century, when times for the poor were very difficult, these people made up only a small percentage of the population as a whole.

Even so, there were periods when life was very difficult for those at the bottom of society. In more prosperous times poorer people would eat a diet of pottage, thickened with grain (usually oats or barley), bread, meat, dairy products and fruit or vegetables which they grew themselves. If the harvest was poor, the price of grain would go up and so a greater percentage of their incomes would be spent on it. Bread was the cheapest way of filling your stomach, so grain had top priority when it came to buying food.

Wheat was considered the best grain but if the wheat harvest failed then poor people would be driven to buying cheaper grains such as oats, barley or rye. Unfortunately, the prices of these would go up as demand increased. The result would be that there was less money available for anything but basic grain and poorer people could become malnourished. In times of particular shortage the poorest might even be reduced to eating unsuitable food, which could bring on disorders of the intestines. This was a very real danger. Food was far more expensive in real terms than it is today and so cost a far greater percentage of people's incomes. For example, Antwerp was a very prosperous city at the end of the sixteenth century and yet about four-fifths of the average income there was spent on food.[5] A fairly small increase in prices could therefore lead to the poorest people having to give up eating the more expensive foods like dairy produce and meat.

Assuming that the harvests had been good and there were no shortages just how healthy was the Tudor diet? What you ate obviously varied according to your pocket, but moderately well-off Tudors at least seem to have eaten quite well. In years when they could afford plenty of 'white meat', that is, dairy products, most people would have eaten fairly well. Cheese was consumed in great quantities, as was butter. Butter was used as a cooking fat and it was eaten on its own too. Sailors in Henry VIII's navy were given butter to eat on days when they were not given cheese. Andrew Boorde talks of the French eating it after meals and jokes of the Dutch eating it all the time.[6] The whey left over from making cheese would also have been drunk. All these products provide amino-acids, which help growth and maintenance of the body.[7] There would also have been plenty of protein in a such a diet, especially combined with the protein from the grain in pottage and bread. In times of shortage, when poorer people ate fewer dairy products, there was a real danger that they might lack vitamins A and D. Vitamin A is found in green vegetables and in animal fat. In diets which do not include enough green vegetables the animal fat becomes very important.

In Tudor terms people would have been eating this fat in the form of dairy products and in the yolk of eggs, but if the animals or hens were not getting enough vitamin A themselves, these products would not contain much vitamin A either. The vitamin A content of dairy products is best when the cows are out at pasture and this is one reason why vitamin A deficiency would have been more likely in early spring when the cows had been kept inside during the winter. The spring would also be the most likely time for deficiency to be felt, as excess vitamin A can be stored in the liver for a few months, so the problem would not have developed in the first few months of winter.

Vitamin A deficiency leads to what is known as 'night blindness', when a person passing from a bright light to a dark one cannot see properly for a time. As the deficiency gets worse eye problems develop, and the lids of the eyes become swollen and sore and the surface of the eyeball dry. In really severe cases the cornea of the eye develops ulcers and if there is no treatment, blindness can develop. Continued deprivation of vitamin A also leads to a general weakening of the immune system. Abscesses and sores may appear.

People might also have suffered from vitamin C deficiency, at least during the winter. The dietary advice of the time was generally that raw fruit was not to be trusted. This was a piece of advice which dated from the time of Galen, who thought that fruit brought on fevers. He stated that his own father had lived to be a hundred as a result of never eating it.[8] Given that too much fresh fruit can cause diarrhoea it was perhaps not surprising that people thought it had a link with dysentery and other stomach disorders.

We do not know to what extent even wealthy people followed this advice. The portrait of Lord Cobham and his family dining shows the family happily ending their meal with raw fresh fruit. We certainly don't know that poorer people followed the advice at all. They would generally not have been as well educated and may not have been as aware of 'expert opinion' as the more affluent. In any case, they might not have cared. They certainly grew fruit like apples, pears and cherries so they would have eaten the fruit. Whether they ate it raw or cooked is unknown.

The other problem was that there wasn't very much in the way of fruit or fresh green vegetables available during the winter whether people were eating them or not. Some apples did keep a reasonable amount of time if stored properly but by the spring it is possible that many people were close to developing scurvy.

The very large amount of wholemeal bread eaten by ordinary people, coupled with all the ale and beer that they drank, must have been a more than ample source of vitamin B. Beer would also have been an excellent source of riboflavin.

Those who ate best from the health point of view were probably the artisans and tradespeople who lived in towns. They tended to be better off than the bulk of the population, who lived in the countryside. They were more likely to have a good diet even in times when harvests were unproductive. On the other hand, they were poor enough to be still likely to eat more fresh fruit and vegetables than the wealthy did.

William Brooke, tenth earl of Cobham and his family. The Brookes are pictured finishing their meal, happily eating raw fruit whatever medical opinion of the day might have said. (The Marquess of Bath: photograph Courtauld Institute of Art)

The very wealthy person's diet, ironically, does not seem to have been as healthy as a poorer person's. Wealthy people ate between two and three pounds of either fish or meat in a day, but this was not necessarily unhealthy in itself. Traditional Eskimo and Tartar diets both consisted of similar amounts of meat. The problem was the lack of fresh fruit and vegetables.

It certainly wasn't true that wealthy people never ate either of these things but they don't seem to have been eating them in large enough quantities to keep them truly healthy. Many of them were probably deficient to some extent in vitamin C.

Wealthy people might also be eating large amounts of sugar, which of course did their teeth no good. The luxurious banqueting food mentioned elsewhere was definitely not for everyday use, but sugar was used on a daily basis in cooking. 'I pray you, forget not my sugar, for if you do you are like to have but sour sauce', Sabine Johnson wrote to her husband while he was abroad.[9] It was also considered healthy to eat sugar. 'Sugar is a thynge verye temperate and nourysshynge' was how Thomas Elyot described it.[10] Sugar was known to be bad for the teeth but that didn't stop people eating it any more than it does today.

One section of the population which was particularly likely to suffer from bad diet was the very young. The best food for an infant is breast milk, especially as it contains its mother's antibodies which will help it fight disease.

Wealthy women did not breastfeed their children. They wanted to have as many children as possible to ensure heirs for the family and breastfeeding a child could delay the next pregnancy. In exceedingly wealthy households, like those of royalty or nobility, the wet-nurse would come and live with the child rather than vice versa. Under those circumstances it was unlikely that the child would be neglected. In other cases the child was often sent to live with the wet-nurse until it was weaned, and that was when danger could develop. The wet-nurse might not take proper care of the child and it might die as a result.

Ironically, less-well-off children stood a better chance of survival. They were fed by their own mothers, which was really the best nourishment they could have been given at the time. Problems really developed if the mother died or if she was incapable of feeding her baby, perhaps because she was undernourished herself. There really was no good alternative to breast milk. Milk from other animals was tried, as was 'pap', a mixture of bread and milk which was made to look like breast milk. The chances were that an infant deprived of human breast milk would die.

The problem was not only whether or not the food given contained the right nutrients. A baby's immune system is very weak and the antibodies it takes in with its mother's milk are vital to it. Given the less hygienic conditions of the time a child lacking these antibodies would have little chance of survival.

Children were fed on breast milk for much longer than they tend to be today. Two years of being breastfed was not uncommon. The food given to a child afterwards varied enormously, depending on its economic circumstances. For most children there must simply have been no other food available than the pottage and bread that the rest of the family ate, so they would have been weaned directly on to that. For the wealthy child a rather more refined diet was recommended.

Jacques Guillemeau, doctor to the French Court, wrote a book entitled *The Happy Deliverie of Women*. It was translated into English in the early seventeenth century and was much read by its new English audience. He strongly advised that a mother should feed her own child and also thought that when the child was weaned it should be fed first on sops of bread or gruel. It was then to be given a leg of chicken with most of the flesh removed so as to encourage the child to gnaw at the bone. After this the child was to progress to capon or partridge minced and mingled with broth. A luxurious diet indeed.[11]

The health of the population depended not only on what they were eating but also on the quality of the food. Food adulteration was unfortunately a problem even for the Tudors.[12]

The mainstay of life for most people was bread which was very strictly regulated by law. Not only was the price of bread carefully controlled but also the contents in terms of mixtures of grain allowed. Selling underweight bread was another offence.

By no means everyone baked their own bread even in the sixteenth century. Ovens were expensive to run, as they used a large amount of fuel. They were usually built into a wall and sometimes, especially in towns, people did not have enough space for one. Loaves could be cooked on hot stones or on irons but the fact that so many bakers existed shows that many people obviously either chose to, or had to, buy bread.

Adulterating bread in various ways seems to have been a fairly common practice. Sometimes bread was baked with sand to make it heavier. Sometimes bad flour was mixed with good, or rye, barley, beans and oats were all mixed together in bread which was supposed to be made of wheat. Here is an extract from the 'Ordinary' of the Bakers of York for the year 1589:

> And nowe whereas my Lord Mayor and this court are informed that dyvers bakers of this cittye viz Raulfe Hardye, John Garther and Richard Clerke have of late used to sell course meal to the powre of this Cittye and that they have mingled and made up this same with branne, chesal [grit] and such like stuffe and further they do commonlye use to bye evill corne and to mingle Rye Barley Beanes and Oates together, and do grind the same into meale and do sell the same to the poore . . . it is this daye agreed that from henceforth no manner of baker or bakers whatsoever within this Cittye shall grind any manner of corne or graine whatsoever into meale to the intent to sell the same in meale, nor that the said bakers sell or course to be anye manner of meale Wheat meale and beane meale being onlye expected upon paine to forfeit xl*s* for every offence.[13]

Evidence such as this must be put in context. There were large numbers of bakers in every town and by no means all of them were practising such deceit. The evidence of the courts shows the sort of tricks the dishonest were getting up to and does suggest that you had to be careful where you bought your bread, but it does not mean that all bought Tudor bread was of poor quality.

However, the standard of ale and beer sold in Tudor England does seem to have been questionable. John Skelton's poem about Elynour Rummynge, quoted in chapter four, was not the only complaint written about alewives. Andrew Boorde berates both alewives and bakers in his *Dyetary of Health*:

> God may sende a man goode meate, but the devyll may sende an evyll cooke to dystrue it, wherefore, gentyll bakers, sophystycate not your breade made of pure whete, yf you do, where evyl ale-brewers and ale wyves, for their evyl brewyng and evyl measure shuld clacke and ryng their tankards at dymm mys dale, I wold you shuld shake out the remnaunt of your saches standynge in the Temnes up to the harde chynne and iii ynches above, that whane you shake your eares as a spanyell that veryly commeth out of the water . . .[14]

Boorde had obviously had enough of the fraudulent practices of both trades. His desire to see the bakers and brewers ducked in the Thames is very apt as ducking was a punishment given to members of both trades who broke the law by selling sub-standard produce.[15]

Peppercorns from the wreck of the *Mary Rose*. (Mary Rose Trust no. 93-5004 TC)

It was not only everyday foods such as bread and beer that were likely to be sub-standard. Ever since the Middle Ages the Company of Grocers, which imported spices, had employed a 'garbler', whose job it was to check the standard of spices being sold. The city records give some idea of the tricks he had to look out for: fresh new spices might be mixed with old ones to make up weight; the sacks containing the spices might be damped down to make them heavier, as were the spices themselves in some cases. The spices often contained grit, dirt, etc., which inevitably found its way into the sacks as they made their long journey from the East. It was the job of the seller to sieve out such impurities before passing on the spices. The buyer, however, would have to take care that this had been done before he parted with any money. He also had to check that the seller had not taken the opportunity to make up the weight with added gravel and such rubbish as pepper stalks.[16]

General standards of food hygiene must also have played a part in people's health. It is impossible to know what the general standards of cleanliness were, although the Tudors were well aware that there was a link between dirt and disease. They tended to think that the bad smells caused by rotting matter and so on were the real problem, which was a reasonable conclusion at the time. This did mean that they regarded cleanliness as a virtue, even if for the wrong reason. Andrew Boorde's advice on building a house and keeping it clean shows that the Tudors were interested in cleanliness. Thomas Elyot, too, considered 'moch people in smal roome living sluttishely' as one potential cause of disease.[17]

Whether keen on cleanliness or not, it would have been hard for most people to keep their kitchens clean. Earth floors were usual at this time and keeping wooden utensils hygienic is difficult. Not surprisingly perhaps there was a genuine fear of death by poisoning among the very wealthy, which gave rise to the elaborate tasting ceremonies which formed part of formal meals. Deliberate poisoning certainly did take place but more often food poisoning rather than a malicious act was to blame.

There was one type of food poisoning which was fairly common in continental Europe, although not in England. This was ergot poisoning, caused by eating rye heavily infected with the fungus *claviceps purpurea*. The gangrenous form starts with an intense burning sensation and itching skin and so it is known as St Anthony's Fire or Holy Fire. As the disease progresses gangrene develops in toes, fingers or even in whole limbs. Another form of the disease causes convulsive fits. The reason it does not seem to have been a problem in England was that although rye was eaten extensively it was not usually eaten on its own. In the south of England it was mixed with barley or wheat and in the north, with barley or oats. As a result the amount of ergot eaten was probably kept at a safe level.[18]

The Tudor diet does seem to have been fairly healthy unless you were a member of a poor family in a time when the harvest had been bad. Even then, fortunately, the chances of dying of actual starvation were rare unless you had the misfortune to be a wandering beggar. The English diet in the sixteenth century was much better than in some other European countries. The average English person lived better than the average French person, for example. The descriptions of England as a land abounding in green pastures and fine, healthy livestock may have been idealized, but they do underline the fact that it was a relatively fortunate nation.

Another significant reason for this was that the Tudors do seem to have concerned themselves with the idea of healthy eating. The idea is not a modern one. The ancient Greeks discussed the concept at some length in their medical treatise and the generations of doctors who followed have all added their own thoughts. By the sixteenth century there was a wealth of opinion on what you should eat to be healthy and why. This included not only the views of the ancient Greeks but those of other esteemed medical minds such as Rhazes, a great Arab doctor, and Avicenna, a Persian who lived at the turn of the tenth century, with the thoughts of Byzantium and ancient Rome thrown in for good measure. If you have ever felt confused by the huge amount of advice on diet available today you will sympathize with the Tudors. A well-to-do Tudor could buy a variety of books giving dietary advice, but following them and working out what exactly he or she should or should not be eating would have been almost a full-time job. Tudor dietary advice sounds exceedingly odd to us today. In order to appreciate the reasoning behind it, it is necessary to have some understanding of how the Tudors thought that the body worked.

The Tudors believed that everything was made up of the four elements of earth, air, fire and water. The earth was considered dry, water was moist, fire was hot and air was cold. Blends of these

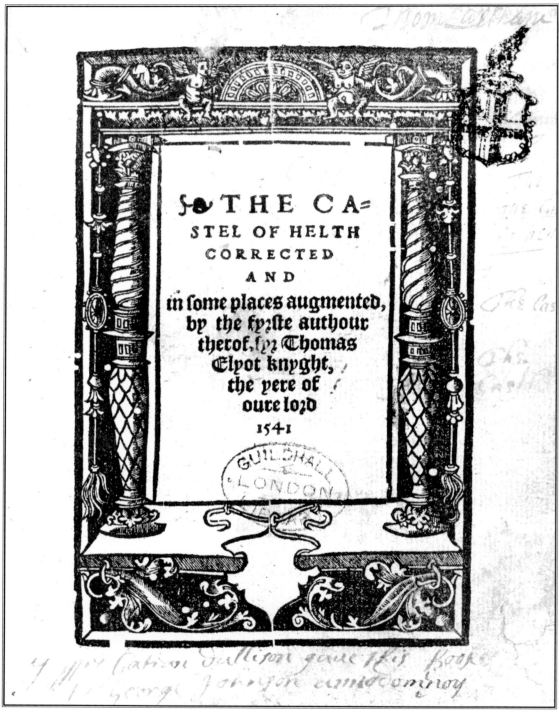

There were plenty of books available on health and fitness even in the sixteenth century. Here is the title page of Sir Thomas Elyot's *The Castel of Helth*. (Guildhall Library, Corporation of London)

elements made up the four basic character types: sanguine (hot and moist), phlegmatic (cold and moist), choleric (hot and dry) and melancholic (cold and dry). These ideas date back to the time of Aristotle. The famous ancient Greek doctor Hippocrates had had very similar ideas, claiming that the body was made up of four 'humours', or liquids, which were blood, phlegm, yellow bile and black bile. As time went on these two ideas became mixed up together so that a sanguine person was considered to have blood as the dominant humour in his or her constitution, while a phlegmatic one had, of course, phlegm. The choleric person's dominating humour was yellow bile and the melancholic person's, black bile.[19]

The different types of constitution or 'complexion' led not only to differences in appearance but also differences in behaviour. Here are the characteristics of the choleric complexion, as described by Sir Thomas Elyot:

> leaness of body
> costiveness [constipation]
> hair black or dark auburn, curled
> visage and skin red as fire or sallow
> hot things harmful to him
> little sleep
> dreams of fire, fighting or anger
> wit sharp and quick
> hardy and fighting
> pulse swift and strange
> urine highly coloured and clear
> voice sharp[20]

This may seem an odd combination of qualities to us but it shows how the humours were thought to dominate everything. The combination that you were born with affected everything from your appearance to your general health and behaviour. It was not just illness which was thought to be caused by an imbalance of humours but also problems such as learning difficulties or sudden and seemingly unexplained outbursts of temper. Urine is mentioned because doctors believed that they could diagnose their patient's condition by examining the urine. Often they did not examine the patients themselves at all; instead a servant might be sent to the doctor's house with their master or mistress's urine sample to save him or her the bother of having to go to visit the doctor.

Tudor medicine was based very much on the ideas of ancient Greece. The authority of the great doctors of antiquity, like Galen and Hippocrates, was quoted like scripture and if a doctor's opinions differed from those of the great men then he would have to be careful how he expressed them. As late as 1559 Dr John Geynes was cited before the Congregated College of Physicians for denying the authority of Galen and had to sign a humble recantation before he was received back.[21]

Medical training was very theoretical, and was based on the study of these classical authorities rather than practical observation. Things were beginning to change, however. It was in the sixteenth century that dissection of dead bodies and the proper study of anatomy began slowly to become part of a doctor's training, and people were starting to question the ancient medical theories. The old views were still generally accepted, though, and the discovery of even such a basic principle as the circulation of the blood still lay some way in the future.

University-trained doctors, although considered the top of the medical profession, comprised only a small percentage of those who practised medicine. These doctors charged very large fees and only the rich could afford them. Further down the social scale there were also the barber-surgeons, who practised surgery and were the people normally called in when blood-letting was thought to be helpful. There were also apothecaries, who did make up prescriptions for doctors but who could also be consulted directly, just like a modern pharmacist.

The person most commonly approached for medical advice was still the woman of the house. Women were brought up to know how to make medicines and how to use them. In a rich household a doctor would be called in for more serious cases but the lady of the house was still expected to deal with minor ailments – and also some not-so-minor ones, judging from the contents of the ladies' commonplace books.[22] However, it was the university-trained doctors, or those like Thomas Elyot who had studied the same texts as the doctors, who wrote the dietary advice books which got into print.

The Tudors were well aware that the moon controlled the tides and so it was felt that the stars influenced the humours of the body in the same way. The study of astrology was a standard part of medical practice, so much so that the publication of astrological predictions and charts became a sideline for many doctors. Andrew Boorde was one of the first people in England to do this, publishing an *Almanacke and Prognostigation* for 1537.

An 'astrological man' such as this was a common illustration in medical textbooks. It explains which parts of the body are governed by which signs of the zodiac. (Samantha Doty)

Letting blood by various means was a favourite treatment at the time. Disease was, after all, thought to be due to an imbalance of the humours so in certain situations it was a logical thing to do. The letting of blood was felt to vary in effectiveness according to the time of the year, as certain parts of the body were believed to be ruled by certain star signs. An 'astrological man', like the one shown above, was a very common illustration in medical texts for this reason.

As the idea of the circulation of blood was not known it was also thought to be important that you let blood from the right place to achieve certain effects. William Bulleyn recommends opening 'the middle vayne of the forehead' for help with forgetfulness, migraine and 'passions of the head'. Leprosy and deafness could be helped by letting blood from the veins behind the ears. As blood was thought to be the 'chief warmer of nature' bloodletting had to be undertaken with care, however. It was thought to be bad for people living in cold places and also for old men, children and pregnant women.[23]

A person's complexion would not only vary according to the mixture of humours but also according to their age. Children and adolescents were thought to be hot and moist, then the body moved into being hot and dry, then finally to being cold and dry as old age came on.[24]

It was not only the human body which was thought to be made up of the four elements. Everything in existence was thought to be created in the same way and so it followed that by studying the composition of vegetables, animals and herbs you could eat those which best balanced the type of constitution you had. Certain types of food were thought to engender certain humours. For example, garlic, onions, leek and mustard were thought to engender choler while salt fish engendered melancholy.[25] It therefore followed that certain foods were healthy for one person to eat, but very bad for another person who had a different complexion.

The health advice books of the time were well aware of this and different diets are recommended according to people's humours. This was Andrew Boorde's advice for the choleric man: 'Choler is hot and dry, wherefore choleric men must abstain from eating hot spices and to refrain from drinking of wine and eating of choleric meat: howbeit choleric men may eat grosser meat than any other complexions, except their education have been to the contrary. Choleric men should not be long fasting.'

A list of food and herbs to purge choler follows this advice.[26]

This makes it sound as if healthy eating, following sixteenth-century rules, was a fairly simple matter. You simply decided what your complexion was and then ate accordingly. That was easier said than done. You had to know the qualities of various foods, something a layman would not necessarily be able to work out for himself. You also had to bear in mind the time of year, because the qualities of food could vary with the seasons. The complexities were such that you could understand why learned men could make such a profitable sideline of writing dietary advice books.

The qualities of foods were not simply 'hot' or 'cold' either, but were divided into different degrees of hot and cold. William Bulleyn explained this by saying 'a lion is hotter than a choleric man: pepper is hotter than cloves', which sums up the thinking of the time very well.[27] It is for this reason that Gerard describes quinces as being 'cold and dry in the second degree', whereas mulberries gathered before they are ripe are cold and dry 'almost to the third degree'.[28]

The degree to which something was hot or cold was only one

Mechanised handwashing, sixteenth-century style. The 'tun' is designed to hold rosewater. The 'wagon' contains a clockwork mechanism which allows it to move along the table, dripping rosewater on to the guests' hands. The mechanism is still in working order. The wagon and tun was presented to the Mercers' Company by William Burde in 1554. (Reproduced by courtesy of the Mercers' Company)

One of the garden pavilions at Montacute House in Somerset. These have a 'lodging chamber' on the top floor but could also be used for banquets. There was also another separate banqueting house at Montacute. (National Trust Photographic Library)

The Tudor stage image. This picture shows an imagined meeting of Francis I and Henry VIII, from the Treaty of Amiens. (Public Record Office, E30/1114)

The kitchen at Buckland Abbey, built by Sir Richard Grenville as part of his conversion of Buckland from a Cistercian Abbey to a private home. (National Trust Photographic Library/George Wright)

The official image of Elizabeth I, as taken from a plea roll dated Easter 1589. The Tudors used court celebrations and festivals as ways of creating and promoting their image. (Public Record Office, KB27/1309)

The elaborate entertainments given by Wolsey to entertain the French ambassadors were part of the negotiations of the Treaty of Amiens, made in 1527. Part of the elaborately illuminated final treaty, now in the Public Record Office, is shown here. (Public Record Office, E30/1109)

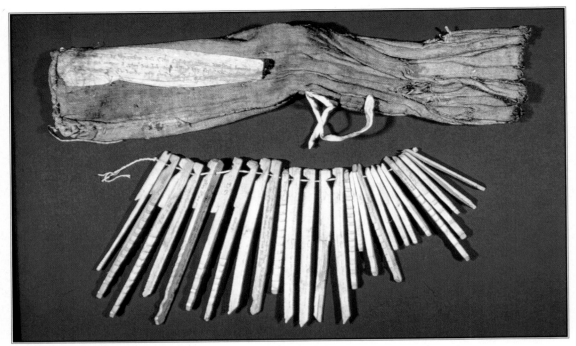

Tally sticks from the Public Record Office. These date from the fourteenth century, but the ones used in the sixteenth century would have looked just the same. (Public Record Office, E101/261/21)

Rock crystal pieces which belonged to Queen Elizabeth I's right-hand man, Cecil, Lord Burghley (1520–98) and his son Robert Cecil (1563–1612). They show just how exquisite and delicate tableware could be in the sixteenth century. (By courtesy of the Marquess of Salisbury)

Maximilian I (above) and Ferdinand I, Archduke of Austria, being invested with the Order of the Garter. (College of Arms, Vincent MS 152, p. 178)

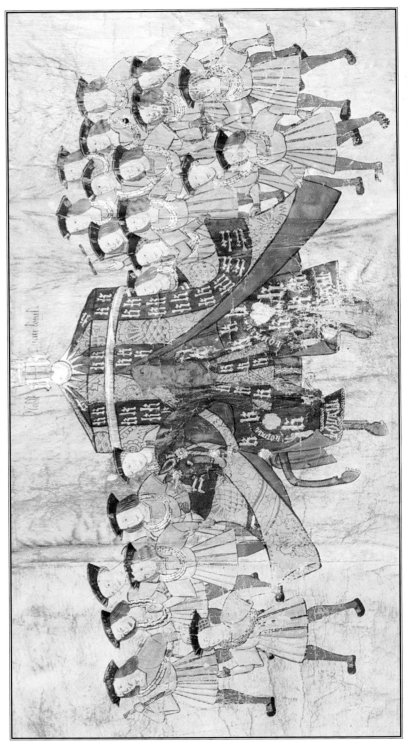

Royal splendour: Henry VIII enters the tiltyard at Westminster in 1511 in the guise of *Cœur Loyal*. The Ks are for Katherine of Aragon, whom he had married in 1509. At this time they were still a young couple in love. (College of Arms, Westminster Tournament Roll, 1511)

complication. Just as the qualities of human bodies varied from youth to old age, so did animals and even fruit. For example, beef from oxen under the age of four was considered by Thomas Elyot to be as nourishing to a choleric man as the more delicate and expensive meat of chickens. Beef from oxen aged over four years was considered good for Englishmen, provided they were healthy, but was liable to engender melancholy.[29] New figs were considered hot and moist, but old ones were only hot in the first degree and dry in the second.

Another factor to be considered was the kind of food that you were used to eating. It was generally assumed that certain nationalities or classes of people could eat things that would be bad for other people simply because they were used to eating them. This was why Andrew Boorde considered that beer was a good drink for the Dutch, but a bad one for Englishmen. He was convinced that ale was our national drink, and should remain so.[30]

Boorde also talks of 'bean butter' which was used in Lent in place of real butter. He describes it as 'food for plowmen to fyl the paunche'.[31] Ploughmen, in his view, were used to such rough country fare and such things were good for them to eat. Thomas Cogan, too, talks of brown bread and butter as being a good breakfast for a countryman, although fine white manchet bread, the most expensive form of bread, was usually that recommended for more gently-bred stomachs.[32]

Generally, healthy foods were those which made 'good juice and good blood'. Expert opinion was divided on exactly what these foods were but usually those which were seen as easily digested were considered good and those hard to digest bad. Thomas Elyot thought hard cheese, old mutton, old swan, black pudding, all raw herbs except lettuce, borage and chicory made bad blood and 'ill juice'. Good foods included well-baked bread, which was neither too old nor too stale and made of pure flour, pigeons, red deer venison, wine drunk in moderate quantities, well-brewed ale or beer six days old and milk drunk on an empty stomach with sugar or mint leaves added.

The order in which dishes were to be eaten could influence their preparation. Some foods were considered best eaten before a meal and others at the end; some could be eaten at either time, but were believed to have different effects according to when they were eaten. Quinces, for example, should be cold and dry if you ate them *before* a meal as they would 'bind and restrain' the stomach. If you cored them, roasted or boiled them and mixed them with clarified honey or

sugar they were then considered useful for stimulating the appetite
and were even thought to keep drunkenness away. If you preferred to
eat your quinces *after* a meal, they would soothe your stomach and
aid digestion.[33]

The time of day at which a meal was taken was another factor for
consideration. Thomas Cogan quotes a proverb which said that
'Butter is gold in the morning, silver at noon and lead at night.'[34]
Eating too much before going to bed, or indeed over-indulging at
any time, was a threat to health. Cogan recommended that dinner
should be at about 11 a.m., which was about four hours after
breakfast. Supper was to be at about 5 p.m., four to five hours after
dinner. Andrew Boorde felt strongly that two meals a day were quite
enough for many men, although labourers could eat three times a
day. 'An houre is suffycyent to syt at dinner and not so long at
supper,' he also warned.[35]

The 'traditional' large British breakfast was not something the
Tudors indulged in. Some did not eat breakfast at all, while those
who did generally enjoyed a light meal of bread and sometimes cold
meat. At Court, only dinner and supper were served, and Thomas
Tusser recommended that servants should not be allowed to sit down
to eat before they had done some work:

> No breakfast of custome provide for to save
> but onely for such as deserveth to have.
>
> No shewing of servant what vittles in store
> shew servant his labour, and show him no more.[36]

The way in which food was cooked could also affect its qualities.
Andrew Boorde was very interested in this idea and had a high
opinion of good cooks: 'A good coke is halfe a physycyon. For the
chefe physycke (the counceyll of a physycyon excepte) doth come
from the kytchyn, wherefore the physycyon and the coke for syche
men must consult together for the preparacion of meate for sycke
men. For yf the physysyon without the coke prepare any meate,
excepte he be very experte, he wyll make a werysse sysshe of meate,
the whiche the sycke can not take.'[37] The principles applied not only
to food intended for the sick. The cooking method used could
counteract the natural qualities of the meat, so that meat which was
dry was best cooked by being boiled, while meat which was moist
was best roasted.[38] Some foods were good when cooked one way but

bad cooked in another. For example, Boorde recommended 'newe reare roasted egges' in the morning, taken with a little salt and sugar, but fried eggs were considered bad for you. If you fancied a poached egg, that would be fine, but it was best to eat it at night.[39]

Thomas Cogan was also of the belief that a good cook was a great asset to good health. Stockfish, the only fish most ordinary people could afford, was not well thought of, yet even such humble and unappetizing food as this could be turned into a healthy meal by an adept cook. Cogan had eaten a stockfish pie 'which hath beene verie good but the goodnesse was not so much in the fishe as in the cookerie which may make that savourie, which is of it selfe unsavourie. And as it is saide a good Cooke can make you good meate of a whetstone, even so it may be that suche fish and flesh as is of it owne nature unwholesome and unpleasant, by the skill of dressing, may be made both wholesome and pleasant.'[40]

A good cook was not the only requirement, however. The health-conscious Tudor was also told to eat according to the season of the year. This was not only because certain foods changed their qualities with the seasons, but because it was felt that certain humours were strongest at certain times of the year: blood increased in spring, phlegm in winter, red choler in summer and yellow choler in autumn.[41] A careful diet would take all this into consideration. Then, as now, there were some foods which were not considered healthy for anyone, whatever their complexion. Again, the authorities, or those who set themselves up as authorities, on healthy eating could not always agree on what these unhealthy items were. Bread baked without yeast, or baked on hot stones, upon irons or before a hearth, was generally considered unhealthy. This was the usual way that poor people cooked bread, since ovens were expensive things to run, so wealthy people probably did not have a high opinion of such bread. To be fair, though, the wafers, cracknels and other fancy biscuits, which were a treat usually reserved for the better-off, were also considered bad. Other matters were not so black and white. Andrew Boorde considered cream a very bad thing to eat while Thomas Cogan praised it.[42] Boorde also goes so far as to contradict Galen over eating pork. Galen praised it, whereas Boorde felt that it was not a healthy meat.

As we have already seen, the condition of the air was another factor which could affect food. The Tudors believed that bad smells caused disease, a reasonable assumption in the days before bacteria were known. Andrew Boorde was particularly keen on the importance of keeping a house clean so as to avoid the build-up of

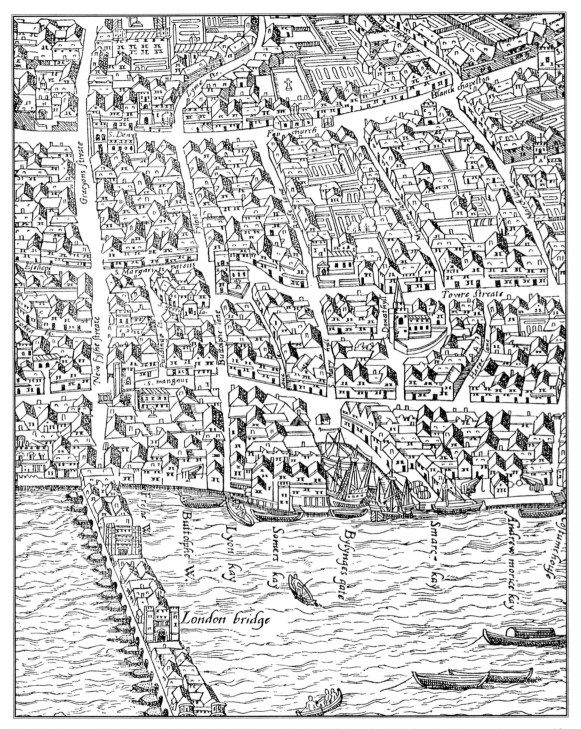

The 'Agas' map of Elizabethan London showing 'Bylynges Gate', the fish market. The barrels sitting on the quay could contain salted fish which was imported in large quantities. (Guildhall Library, Corporation of London)

bad smells. 'Pysse-pots' and 'pyssing in chymnes' were to be avoided so as to keep the house sweet. The buttery, cellar, kitchens and larders in particular were to be kept clean.[43]

Corrupted air was thought likely to make certain plants unsafe to eat. Boorde warned against eating pottage in times of pestilence as the herbs put into it were very likely to have been infected by the bad air.[44] Damp night air and the air near stagnant water was also considered dangerous. Even the stars could cause 'bad air' and this was when plague was liable to break out. Plague was naturally the great fear of the age and the health writers always include some kind of instruction on how to live during times of pestilence. Thomas Elyot advises avoiding heat from either garments or fires and avoiding all hot herbs except onions and chicory. Andrew Boorde suggests closing up windows and doors against the air and not going out, while burning various herbs to fumigate the air. He also gives instructions for making a pomander to ward off disease.[45] Unfortunately there was really very little that anyone, rich or poor, could do to protect themselves against the plague once it had entered their household. Thomas Elyot's suggestion to 'flee from the place corrupted' was no doubt the best advice for the wealthy audience he was writing for.[46]

Diet was seen not only as a way of keeping in good health but also as a way of curing or controlling various diseases if you were unfortunate enough to become ill. This is an idea which would be seen as perfectly respectable today but of course we also have the benefit of other treatments, such as a course of drugs. In Tudor times it often must have been the only thing that doctors could recommend, although we might not regard the particular diet as appropriate today. Andrew Boorde provides various diets for people suffering from everything from asthma to headaches. Those suffering from a consumption (wasting disease), for example, were advised to keep away from sour foods, such as vinegar. They were to avoid eating 'grose meates', which were those considered hardest to digest, like mutton and also food which had been fried. Meats which had been burnt by too much roasting were also to be avoided. Stewed rabbit, pig, chicken stewed and made into a jelly, and rice soaked in almond milk were all recommended.[47]

In Tudor times, despite the vast amount of ink spilt on the subject, healthy eating must only have been a kind of hobby for the well-off. The advice in dietary books was meant for the middle and upper classes, being the only people who could afford to pay for the books in the first place. The diets advocated, containing great quantities of meat and luxuries like sugar and oranges, were as far beyond the reach of the ordinary Tudor as the cost of consulting a university-educated doctor. Most Tudors could only afford the usual pottage, bread and home-grown fruit and vegetables, no matter what the authorities may have been advising.

In some ways, despite the bias towards the wealthy, these books seem quite modern in the advice they give. They definitely take the holistic approach. Not only was it necessary to eat well to remain healthy, but to live in a well-built house set in a well-aired, well-drained location. The house must be clean and well-organized, with the refuse heap and the privies set in a position where they could not damage the health of the occupants. Andrew Boorde regarded this as so important that he devotes several chapters of his book to these ideas. Admittedly, the house he describes is more like a palace than an ordinary home but at least the basic ideas are there.

The need to have a well-balanced life is also put forward in many books of the time. They recommend getting enough, but not too much, sleep. Thomas Cogan, in *The Haven of Health*, also advocates a healthy sex life (the Tudors were far from prudish), although stresses that this must be within the constraints of good Christian marriage. Cogan did not want to be seen as encouraging immorality.[48]

A glimpse into the anxieties of the sixteenth century is provided by Thomas Elyot. What we would call stress today was seen as a threat to health even in the sixteenth century. He warns how 'things of the mind' can affect health and lists among the causes of worry not only loss of goods, frustration at the lack of promotion and general bad luck but also 'the deathe of chylderne'.[49] People often make the assumption that somehow parents did not become too attached to their children because of high child mortality, but the evidence of the time does not support this at all. People felt the loss of their children deeply, but since it was a grief that visited most families at least once, if not more often, it was simply something that they had to learn to cope with.

Thomas Elyot's advice to those who mourned the loss of children was spiritual rather than medical. He reminded them that 'death is the discharge of al griefs and mysteries, and to them that dye well, the fyrst entrie is to the lyfe everlastyne'. This was good advice, as sadly there was little that anyone could do to save their children if they fell seriously ill. This is a stark reminder that whatever the faults of modern medicine, it can produce results beyond the wildest dreams of the Tudors, no matter which diet they chose to follow.

CHAPTER SEVEN

Tableware

If you had been invited to dinner in the sixteenth century your host's tableware would have told you far more about him than it would today. More importantly from your point of view, the specific tableware that you were given would have told you how far up, or indeed far down, the social ladder he thought you were.

By the sixteenth century it was no longer usual for a large household to dine all together in the hall. As early as the fourteenth century William Langland was complaining in *Vision of Piers Plowman* that lords were no longer dining with their households, and this trend obviously continued. At Henry VIII's Court everyone was supposed to eat in hall when the Court was staying at the larger palaces. This habit was known as 'keeping hall'. It was done for the practical reason of making the serving of food so much easier, but Henry VIII's Household Ordinances note that 'sundry noblemen, gentlemen and others, doe much delight and use to dyne in corners and secret places, not repairing to the King's Chamber nor hall, nor to the head officers of the household when the hall is not kept'.[1] This change in dining habits naturally affected table manners and the serving of food. However, for a large-scale feast it was still the custom for the host to put on the most impressive display possible. In this case there were certain things to look out for.

The first thing to note would be your host's buffet. A buffet was a cross between a sideboard and a Welsh dresser, and was also sometimes called a cupboard. It was partially functional and partly for display. It provided storage for certain items that would be in use during the meal, such as the ewers and basins in which the guests would wash their hands. Its other use was to display the host's plate. As mentioned in chapter one, plate was a very powerful status symbol in the sixteenth century. Wealthy families invested huge

A buffet, displaying the
household plate.
(Samantha Doty)

sums in it, so obviously they wanted to show it off. The idea was to
have enough plate to serve your guests at a meal *and* to have a
separate display sitting on your buffet.

On very grand occasions an especially powerful host might make
the point that he had so much plate that he did not need to use his

buffet at all. This is how George Cavendish, a courtier at Henry VIII's Court, described the buffet at Cardinal Wolsey's Hampton Court at a feast in 1527:

> There was a cupboard made for the occasion, in length of the breadth of the lower end of the same chamber, six shelves high, full of gilt plate, very sumptuous and of the newest fashions and upon the lowest shelf, garnished all with plate of clean gold, were two great candlesticks of silver and gilt, most curiously wrought (the workmanship whereof, with the silver, cost three hundred marks)[2] and lights of wax as big as torches burning upon the same. This cupboard was barred in round about that no man might come near it; for there was none of the same plate used or stirred during this feast, there being sufficient plate besides.[3]

It was not only the quantity of the plate that was important. The quality and the style were also indicators of a host's status. Silver gilt, for example, was worth quite a lot more than plain silver. The inventory of Archbishop Parker's goods made in the mid-sixteenth century[4] valued the silver at 4s 8d an ounce, while the silver gilt was valued at 5s 4d. To give a better idea of the size of the price difference, this was at a time when agricultural labourers were being paid 6d a day.[5]

The style of the plate was vital because any ambitious family needed to have the very latest in fashionable silverware. Today we value antiques so highly that it is easy to forget that until the eighteenth century old things were not valued unless they had an important association for a person or institution. Much of the old plate which survives in Oxford and Cambridge colleges, for example, was not treasured down the centuries because it was a fine example of certain types of historic silverware but because it had been donated by an important person, such as the founder of the college or some distinguished member of the college. If a family's silverware was old-fashioned it would imply that they did not have enough money to have it melted down and made into something more up to date. This is why Cavendish took care to point out that Wolsey's plate was all 'of the newest fashions'.

As already discussed, if the family needed cash for some reason plate could be melted down and made into coin. This means that very little Tudor plate survives. For much of his reign, Henry VIII was the richest prince in Europe and his jewel-house inventory lists over eight hundred items of gold and silver plate, but only one piece survives today. This is the medieval royal cup which is now in the British Museum.[6] Hardwick Hall in Derbyshire still contains much of the Tudor furniture that was made for the house, but not a single piece of silver plate listed in the impressive inventory of 1601 survives today.[7]

As a Tudor guest you would therefore have looked carefully at the design of your host's plate. In the earlier part of the sixteenth century you would have expected to find simpler designs, following the old gothic styles which had been in fashion since the fifteenth century. England was still a backwater at this time so these designs remained in use even after continental Europe had started to use Renaissance styles. By the 1530s, though, styles were changing. The influence of Holbein began to be felt. He not only painted portraits but also designed a whole range of items from silver plate and jewellery to fireplaces. A number of continental pattern books, imported from places like Antwerp and Frankfurt began to be used in England and a great number of foreign craftsmen came and settled in London. England began to discover the tastes of continental Europe.

As the century progressed, designs became more and more complicated and the range of decoration increased too. The more elaborate pieces might be enamelled, decorated with niello (a compound of silver and sulphur fired to the surface which looks like black enamel), etched with intricate designs or decorated with a number of other techniques. Unfortunately, although very high-quality items were still being produced, the general quality of silverware was declining. A major reason for this seems to have been that the market for silverware was changing.

The sixteenth century saw quite large changes in society. What we would now think of as the middle classes were becoming much wealthier and much more self-confident. These were people who were making their own way in the world, rather than relying on family money. They made money at trade, the law, and from positions in the expanding government bureaucracy. These people had been able to take advantage of the sale of monastery lands. Land meant wealth in the sixteenth century. It was the most secure investment you could make and owning it also gave you social status. These 'new' families wanted all the symbols of wealth that went with their new position in life, which of course included silverware. Possibly they were more concerned with quantity than quality.

These beakers were made in 1604–5 and were presented to the Mercers' Company by John Bancks. (Reproduced by courtesy of the Mercers' Company)

In the late sixteenth century not only would you have been looking out for more elaborate designs on your host's table, you would also have expected a far greater range of items to be made out of silver. This was owing partly to the greater wealth enjoyed by certain people at the time and partly to the fact that new bullion was pouring into Europe from South America. Tankards made of silver were becoming more commonplace and new items such as spice boxes and spice plates were also appearing. Spice plates[8] were wide, shallow bowls on stems which were in fact used for serving a broad range of foods, from sweetmeats to fruit. Sometimes they were even used as a kind of goblet for serving wine.

All of this assumes that your host was somebody very grand. Even at the end of the sixteenth century silver was beyond the reach of most people. The cheaper substitute was pewter, which was usually an alloy of copper and tin. English pewter was highly valued, as the quality of the alloy was very carefully controlled and the workmanship used to create pewter goods was often as fine as that used on silver. William Harrison spoke very highly of English pewter in *Description of England*: 'In places beyond the sea a garnish of good flat English pewter or an ordinary making . . . is esteemed almost so precious as the like number of vessels that are made of fine silver.'[9] He also praises the skill of English pewterers, enthusing that 'they are grown unto such exquisite cunning that they can in manner imitate by infusion any form or fashion of cup, dish, salt, bowl or goblet which is made by goldsmith's craft, though they be never so curious, exquisite and artificially forged'.[10] This was not just a case of a patriotic Englishman exalting his own country's skills. Foreign visitors also spoke highly of English metalwork. Andreas Franciscus, visiting London in 1497, wrote: 'The working in wrought silver, tin or white lead is very expert here, and perhaps the finest I have ever seen.'[11]

Harrison also describes how widespread the use of pewter had become, and how even farmers who had at one time done little more than scrape a living were now able to use pewter plates and even afford silver salts.[12] The price of pewter must still have put it well beyond the reach of much of society, though. The sixteenth century was certainly no golden age. Certain classes in society did indeed flourish but it was a bad time for those at the bottom who found their standard of living decreasing. One estimate, based on inventories, is that by the middle of the sixteenth century about half the households in England were using pewter,[13] which meant of course that about half the population could not afford it. People at the lower end of society would have found that a single substantial item of pewter would have cost an entire day's wages.

According to Harrison, pewter was usually bought by the 'garnish', or a set consisting of twelve platters, twelve dishes and twelve saucers. The saucers were little, bowl-like dishes used for serving the wide variety of sauces which usually accompanied meat. This must have meant that a large quantity of pewter was in use in the sixteenth century, but as pewter is even softer than silver, hardly any of this tableware survives today. It was also quite usual to take your old, worn pewter back to the pewterer to be melted down when you were buying new pieces, as the price of the metal would be taken off the cost of the new items.[14]

Pottery was also used by the Tudors. The kind of pottery used in the kitchen generally had a red glaze but the usual tableware pottery for the less well off had a green glaze. Today it is known as Tudor greenware and was produced in England in large quantities. The better-quality pottery was imported from the Rhineland. Made of salt-glazed earthenware, it was very highly decorated, with designs made of the same earthenware as the pot itself. The decoration was mass produced using moulds, but it was very high quality even so. It was through the popularity of this ornamentation that many ordinary people were introduced to the fashions of the Continent so this pottery played a considerable part in the development of the decorative arts of the time.[15]

There was also a fashion in England for mounting such pottery with silver. Etienne Perlin commented in 1558 that 'the English use much beer, both double and single strength and drink not in glasses, but in earthenware jugs, whose handles are of silver and also the lids, and this is what is done in houses where they are fairly well to do'.[16] An example of this type of jug is shown on page 52.

In the late sixteenth century blue and white porcelain was imported from China, but it was incredibly rare and a great luxury. Delftware copied the style and developed as a cheaper and more accessible alternative. It is earthenware enamelled with tin. It did not necessarily come from Delft, but the name was used here because the technique reached England via Holland. In 1571 two Flemish potters called Jacob Jansen and Jasper Andries[17] sent a petition to Queen Elizabeth asking for permission to settle on the banks of the Thames. They may well have been the first producers of delftware in London. However, delftware only really became popular in the seventeenth century.

Once you had taken stock of your host's tableware it was time to start looking at the items provided at your own place. The first thing to look out for was the ceremonial salt cellar. All the tables would have been provided with salt cellars, but these would have been little bowls and were there purely to ensure that all the diners had salt to put on their meal. The ceremonial salt cellar was all part of the status game.

The ceremonial salt would stand by the place of the most important diner, who would of course be seated at the top table at a feast. This gives us the origin of the expression sitting 'above' or 'below' the salt. Despite the importance of these salt cellars, however, we know very little about how they looked, as so few survive that it is difficult to generalize. The pair of hourglass-style salts which were donated by Margaret Beaufort to her foundation of Christ's College, Cambridge, do survive and they are certainly impressive. The

Goldsmith's Company of London in 1520 owned six chased salts, three of them large, weighing 40 oz each, and three smaller ones weighing 15 oz.[18] The inventory made at the death of Henry VIII's illegitimate son, the Duke of Richmond, contains a variety of salts, including a gold one weighing 25 oz.[19] The ceremonial salt was clearly a piece of plate aimed to impress.

The next item to study was your drinking vessel. If your cup had been provided with a cover it was another sign that your host saw you as someone worth honouring. Cups with covers were kept for the master of the house and the most important guests. Sets of cups usually came with at least one cover to allow for this.[20]

Cups were such a status symbol that they were often very elaborately decorated, like the Leigh Cup (see Frontispiece), which belongs to the Mercers' Company. They were not all made of precious metal, though, as glass was also highly prized. Henry VIII owned over six hundred glass objects, including 'iii standing Cuppes of Blewe glasses wf covers to theym, paynted and guilte'.[21] In the late fifteenth and early sixteenth centuries glass was often brightly coloured and covered with gilt and enamelled ornamentation, so that King Henry was following a widespread fashion. Examples exist in a wide range of colours, from purple to emerald green. As the sixteenth century progressed Venetian glass, which tended to set the fashion for other glass, gradually became lighter and less coloured. A fashionable host by this time would have wanted to provide his guests with either highly engraved clear glass or perhaps drinking vessels made of 'ice glass', which was rolled over water while it was being blown. The technique produced cracks in the glass which looked just like ice. Certainly Philip II of Spain, husband of Mary Tudor, loved this type of glass and in 1564 he had no fewer than sixty-five fine pieces of Venetian ice glass at his palace of El Prado, including glasses and decanters.[22]

William Harrison was somewhat scathing of this fashion for glass: 'It is a world to see in these our days, wherein gold and silver most aboundeth, how that our gentility, as loathing those metals (because of the plenty), do now generally choose rather the Venice glasses, both for our wine and beer, than any of those metals or stone wherein beforetime we have been accustomed to drink; but such is the nature of man generally that it most coveteth things difficult to be attained.' He then goes on to explain that Venetian glass is beyond the pocket of most people so that they have to buy glass made in England 'but in fine all go one way, that is, to shards at the last, so that our great expenses in glass . . . are worst of all bestowed in mine opinion, because their pieces do turn unto no profit'.[23] He certainly had a point. Glass was hardly the good investment that plate was.

As glass became more fashionable, glassworks were set up throughout Europe. As early as the fifteenth century 'forest glass' was being made in the Weald of Kent but this certainly did not match Venetian glass in quality. Fine glass does not seem to have been made in England until Queen Elizabeth's time. This, of course, meant that Henry VIII's glassware must have been imported, making it an even more impressive luxury.

It is unlikely that you would find anything set for you beside your drinking vessel and your trencher. Matching sets of silver cutlery still lay a long way in the future, only really becoming standard among wealthy families in the late seventeenth and early eighteenth centuries. Sets of spoons certainly existed, and were often given as christening gifts, but it was not usual for all the guests to be provided with cutlery. You would expect to bring your own cutlery with you to the table.

Forks were very rare in England in the sixteenth century. In the inventory of the royal jewel house taken in 1574 there were only thirteen silver forks.[25] They were used for serving sticky items, especially sweetmeats, or for helping to steady meat while it was being carved, rather than for eating. Eating with a fork was an Italian fashion which did not reach England until the late seventeenth and early eighteenth centuries. Even in 1617 the traveller Thomas Coryat was quite fascinated by this odd habit when he was travelling in Italy. This is how he recorded it:

I observed a custom in all those Italian Cities and Townes through which I passed, that is not used in any other country that I saw in my travels, neither doe I thinke that any other nation of Christendome doth use it, but only Italy. The Italian and also most strangers that are commorant in Italy do alwaies at their meales use a little forke when they cut their meate. For while with their knife which they hold in one hande they cut the meate out of the dish, they fasten their forke, which they hold in their other hand upon the same dish, so that whatsoever he be that sitting in the company of any others at meate, should unadvisedly touch the dish of meate with his fingers, from which at all the table doe cut, he will give occassion of offence unto the company, as having transgressed the lawes of good

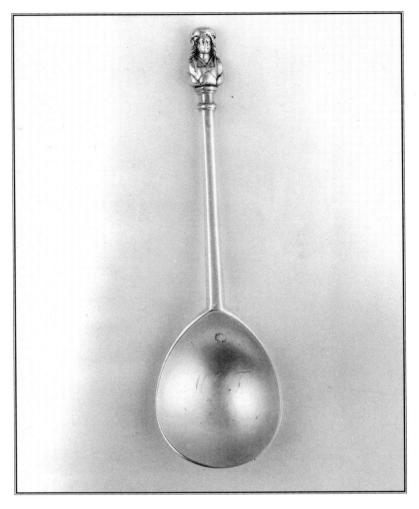

Spoons were personal items in the sixteenth century. Institutions such as the London livery companies often had them made up with the company badge or patron saint decorating the knop. Here is an example, made in 1578, from the collection of the Company of Mercers. The crowned maiden's head is the badge of the company. (Reproduced by courtesy of the Mercers' Company)

manners in so much that for his error he shall be at the least brow beaten, if not reprehended in wordes. . . . The reason of this curiousity is, because the Italian cannot by any means indure to have his dish touched with fingers, feeling all mens fingers are not alike cleane.[26]

Clearly to an Englishman the habit of eating food with a fork seemed very odd indeed.

Though forks were foreign, spoons most definitely were not. They held a special place for the Tudors as prized personal possessions and were made in a bewilderingly wide range of styles. The basic spoons were all made alike, with a wide bowl on a narrow stem, but the

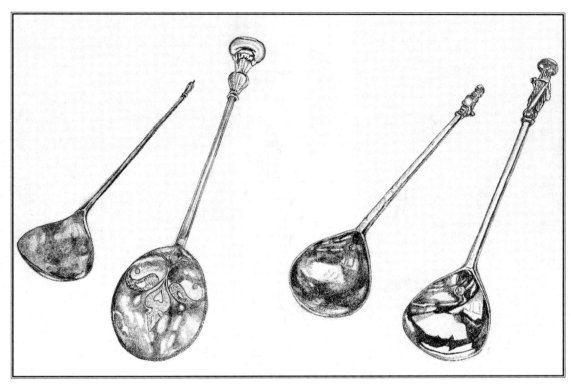

Sixteenth-century spoons. The plain base metal spoon on the far left is of the type that most ordinary people would have used. The three decorative spoons are luxury ones made of silver. (Julie Anne Hudson)

decoration at the end of the handle could be anything from a statue of an apostle to a woodwose (a kind of wood spirit). Henry VIII's jewel house contained sixty-eight gold spoons and 'xij silver Spones wt Columynes at the endes' and even 'a spoone of gold with a steele chased and arounde knoppe having a dyamounte sett in the end'.[27] Even the London livery companies had special designs of spoons. For example, the Inn Holders had spoons with St Julian, their patron saint, on the end.[28] The spoon shown on page 100 still belongs to the Mercers' Company and shows its company badge of the maiden's head.

Relatively large numbers of spoons survive, partly because they contained only about 4 oz of silver each and so were not really worth much as scrap. They also survive because they had strong sentimental value to the Tudors. As personal items they were valued in much the same way that we might value our personal items of jewellery today. They were often left in wills for this reason, and also because if someone did own anything of value, it was likely to be a spoon or set of spoons. Christine Burgh, the former prioress of Nunkilling Abbey

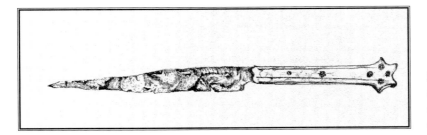

Sixteenth-century knife complete with wooden handle, of the type that most people would have used.

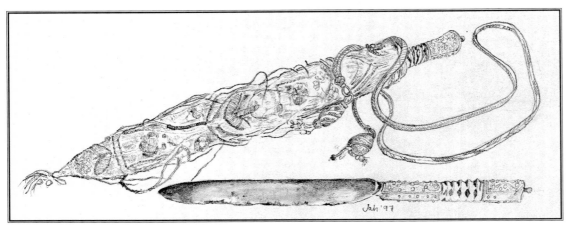

Luxury cutlery from the late sixteenth century. These knives have amber handles with silver pliqué work, a world away from the plain wooden-handled knife above. The elaborate case in which they would have been carried is also shown. It is decorated with silver thread. (Julie Anne Hudson)

in Yorkshire, died in 1566. Her entire estate was worth only £14, and 20s' worth of this was the value of her six silver spoons. They were to be divided up between the beneficiaries of her will.[29]

Even so simple an item as a silver spoon was beyond the reach of most people. In the mid-sixteenth century it would have cost around 4s, which was a week's wages for someone working even in the highly paid building trade.[30] Most people would have owned pewter spoons, or ones made of horn if pewter was too expensive.

Eating knives looked rather like a modern cooking knife, with a leaf-shaped blade. The leaf shape gave the knife a point which was useful for spearing food out of serving dishes. It was, however, the height of bad manners to put your knife in your mouth, just as it still is today. The food would have been removed from the knife and put into the mouth with your fingers.

Grand households did own sets of knives for guests to use but it was more usual to have to bring your own knife to the table. As knives were personal items etiquette books remind diners that it is their duty to see that their knife is in a fit condition to bring to

The Wyndham Ewer and Basin, now in the British Museum, illustrate the elaborate ewers and basins found in great households in the sixteenth century. (Copyright British Museum)

table. 'When ye be set, keep your own knife clean and sharp, that so ye may carve honestly your own meat,' cautions *The Babees Book*, which was written[31] in 1475, a warning which was repeated in other books. Stainless steel was not known at the time and knife blades required careful looking after. They needed to be cleaned frequently to stop them becoming rusty.

Once the meal began you would have had an opportunity to take stock of yet another piece of your host's tableware: the ewer and basin. Guests' hands were washed before and after the meal and also between courses, often in scented water. As all the guests' hands would be washed, and not just those of the most honoured visitors, great houses often owned several ewers and basins. The Duke of Richmond's inventory includes two gilded ewers and five parcel gilt (i.e. partially gilded) ones.[32] Ewers were usually left on the buffet when they were not in use and so were very much display items, like the silver gilt ewer and basin which still survives at Corpus Christi college, Cambridge, and the Wyndham Ewer (above).

Now that you were ready to begin eating it was time to consider your table manners. In a very status-conscious world, table manners were a way of showing off your good breeding, so you had to get them right. As they were quite complicated, they deserve a chapter of their own.

CHAPTER EIGHT

Table Manners

Once the meal began it was time to start thinking of your table manners. The modern idea of the Tudors throwing their food around and wiping their hands on their clothes would have shocked sixteenth-century diners. As clothing was far more expensive at this time it was a matter of logic that table manners were designed so as to allow you to eat without spoiling your clothes. This was particularly important in court circles, where extremes of dress would be found. Elaborately embroidered frills at the wrist were in fashion in the sixteenth century, and for a short while it was even the fashion to wear wrist ruffs. It would have been difficult to have played the part of the elegant courtier if you could not eat your dinner without getting sauce everywhere.

Table manners cannot, of course, be taken in isolation; they are just one aspect of manners. In the sixteenth century there was a belief that a truly well-mannered lady or gentleman should look as if they could do everything elegantly without the slightest effort, as books such as Castiglione's *Courtier* depicted. Great men were expected to put on lavish displays of wealth, but to behave, at least in public, as if their wealth meant nothing to them. Grabbing large quantities of food, stuffing your mouth full and spilling everything would hardly have conveyed the desired image.

The Tudors did not use the word 'etiquette'. It did not exist at the time. Instead they used the word 'courtesy'. The idea was that the way you did anything demonstrated your upbringing, and every act was supposed to show due consideration for others and respect for God. This was why one book, *The Little Children's Little Book*, starts by suggesting that courtesy came to earth 'when Gabriel hailed our Lady by name'. Table manners were seen as part of a whole code of behaviour considered suitable for a well-bred Christian.

The courtesy books always devote huge sections to describing how to eat politely. They all say much the same things. Some instructions are very basic indeed, such as reminders not to pick your ears or your nose at table, so perhaps in reality table manners were not all that gracious by our standards. The books do copy considerably from each other, however, so maybe these warnings were largely conventional. The basic aim, then as now, was to eat as tidily and gracefully as possible. Tudor meals were also used to remind everyone of their place in the social hierarchy, so there were rules to be observed.

Although private dining was becoming more usual, especially for grander people, dining could still be a public occasion for the less important members of a household. In more humble households dining might well have been rather cramped as everyone tried to fit around the table. Table manners were designed to take this lack of space into account.

Tudor tables would have been covered with tablecloths, varying from very coarse to very fine linen, depending on how important the diners were. It was important to keep the tablecloth clean:

> Meat nor drink thou not spill
> But set it down, both fair and still
> Keep thy cloth clean thee beforn
> And bear thee so thou have no scorn.[1]

Often you would also have been given a table napkin, which Erasmus stated should be placed over your left shoulder or left wrist.[2] You were expected to use the napkin, as the courtesy books are full of reminders to keep yourself clean. This was particularly important as you might be sharing your cup with the person sitting next to you, and they would hardly want your grease and crumbs: 'Wipe your mouth before you drink lest it foul the edges of the cup, and keep your fingers, your lips and your chin clean if you would win a good name.'[3] More good advice was to 'Lay not thy elbow nor thy fist/Upon the table whilst thou eat'st',[4] as it was usual to eat off trestle tables, which might not be very stable.

For most Tudors the correct way to drink was to take the cup in both hands. This made good sense because if someone were to knock your elbow when you were drinking you would be less likely to spill anything. In very well-to-do circles the rules were slightly different, as drinking vessels would not be left on the table but would be called for only when wanted. Harrison notes that drinking vessels 'are seldom set on the table, but each one, as necessity urgeth, calleth for

Sir Henry Unton dining in about 1596. Note how the diners have their table napkins folded over their wrists or over their shoulders and how the food is carefully laid out in a symmetrical pattern on the table. (By courtesy of the National Portrait Gallery, London)

a cup of such drink as he listeth to have, so that when he hath tasted of it, he delivered the cup up again to someone of the standersby, who, making it clean by pouring out the drink that remaineth, restoreth it to the cupboard from whence it came'.⁵ Harrison commends this habit, seeing it as a way of stopping people getting drunk, but he also comments that the habit is not used in noblemen's halls (where most of the household would be dining), 'neither in any man's house commonly under the degree of knight or esquire of great revenues'.⁶ Obviously it was only practical to work this system where there were plenty of servants to see to the diners' wishes.

Market hall from Titchfield in Hampshire, now at the Weald and Downland Open Air Museum. The open arcade at ground level was where the market was held, while the room above was used as a council chamber. The building also incorporates a 'cage' or lock-up for offenders. Little local markets were where all the small-scale buying and selling went on, but for luxury items you would need to go to a town. (Alison Sim)

Most Tudors ate out of communal dishes, which is another reason for many of the instructions given in courtesy books. Most meals were served in portions (or messes) designed to serve four people, the largest number who could conveniently share a dish. The more important diners, who would sit at the top table, usually shared with only one other person. As at many weddings today, they only sat

107

along one side of the table, so it would have been difficult for more than two of them to share a dish. Tudor manners were designed to make sharing these dishes as civilized as possible. It was only very grand diners who could expect their own serving dishes, which of course would remind everyone present just how important these people were.

The meal would usually start with the Tudor mainstay, pottage. This would be eaten from a communal bowl, which is why there are so many reminders in courtesy books that it is the height of bad manners to leave your spoon in the dish, thus making it harder for the other diners to help themselves. 'Do not put your spoon in the dish or on the edge of it, as the untaught do,' one book instructs its readers.[7]

It goes on to advise: 'Do not put the meat off your trencher into the dish, but get a voider and empty it into that.' The voider was a special dish where waste food could be put, while a trencher was used in Tudor times rather like a modern plate. During the Middle Ages these had been made of four-day-old bread and for much of the sixteenth century bread trenchers were still used, as can be seen in the picture of Sir Nicholas Unton dining. Wooden ones were also beginning to be used[8] and some houses even used pewter. You would take meat from the communal dish, dip it into one of the sauces provided in the saucers mentioned earlier, and then put the piece of meat into your mouth. The trencher could be used as a halfway stage between the two, although it was very bad mannered to pile it high with food as this would make it look as though you were also trying to grab your messmates' share. Putting your waste back into the communal dish rather than into the voider would indeed have been a disgusting habit.

Constant reminders are also given about that other communal dish, the salt. As it was common to dip meat into the saucers, it would have been understandable had guests thought to dip their meat in the salt too as it would also have been served in little bowls. Obviously the salt would soon have become objectionable, so diners were often advised to help themselves to the salt with their knives and to transfer it from the blade to their food. The wooden trenchers were provided with a little round indentation in the top right-hand corner where the salt could be put.

Eating from the common dishes was not a free-for-all. As explained in the introduction, seating at meals was arranged according to rank and so the most important person sharing the mess would help themselves first, and so on through the group of four.

This not only made for civilized dining, but also reminded everyone of their own and others' social place. 'If thy child be set with his betters, let his hand be last in the dish. And that he do it not at all, unless he be first bidde,' warns Richard Weste, in his *School of Virtue*.[9]

Period films usually make great play of showing people picking up hunks of meat, knawing at them and then throwing the bones to the dogs. This definitely was not the case in real life. For one thing, it was the height of bad manners to have your dog with you at meal times. 'Make neither the cat nor the dog your fellow at the table,' warns the *Young Children's Book*.[10] You were also cautioned that you were not to chew the bones like a dog[11] and you were to put them in the voiding dish, not on the floor.[12] If you were dining at the top table it was highly unlikely that you would come across bones anyway, as carving the meat was part of the ritual which surrounded dining in public. It was a great honour to be asked to carve, and it was the mark of a gentleman to know how to do it correctly. It was such a mark of good breeding that carving became highly complicated, there being a correct way to tackle each type of meat, and a correct vocabulary to go with it. For example, you 'lifted' a swan but you 'reared' a goose and 'dismembered' a heron.[13] Elaborate sets of carving knives were made to emphasize the importance of the ritual. The Duke of Richmond owned 'a paire of kervyng knives, weing xviij oz'[14] which were made of parcel gilt. Carving was such an important part of good manners that courtesy books of the time are often called 'books of carving'.

An important part of dining, according to period films, was the serving wenches. Unfortunately, they did not exist in the sixteenth century – at least, not in grander households. It cost more to employ men than women, so grand households employed men wherever possible as a status symbol. It was men, rather than women, who served food. Serving food, especially to a very important person, was also considered an honour, which was why knowing how to serve properly was so important in the education of a well-to-do boy.

Despite the delicacy of Tudor manners, some things were allowed which would shock the modern diner. Spitting was certainly permitted, although it had to be done discreetly:

> If spitting chance to move thee so
> thou canst it not forbear
> Remember, do it modestly
> consider who is there.[15]

You were also advised to wipe your hand on your clothes if you had to blow your nose[16] so that other people did not have to look at the result.

The basics of good table manners seem to have remained constant throughout the fifteenth and sixteenth centuries, and probably did not change until forks became common. However, there is a change of emphasis in the books over the period, which echoes the change in society.

Books were still expensive even by the end of the sixteenth century. They were much cheaper than they had been in the days before the printing press, but they were still very much the sort of thing that would have been beyond the reach of ordinary people. They were therefore aimed at the wealthier section of society, the very people for whom life changed most in the fifteenth and sixteenth centuries.

The fifteenth-century courtesy books give instruction to young gentlemen, who were usually brought up in the houses of the rich and powerful. Young boys would have been in the charge of a master, who was responsible for seeing that they learned all they needed to know. The Household Ordinances of Edward IV show these young 'henchmen' as being taught 'to ride cleanly and surely, to draw them also to jousts, to . . . wear their harness to have all courtesy in words, deeds and degrees, diligently to keep them in rules of goings and sittings, after they be of honour'. They learned everything from languages to music and dancing, and the master always sat with them at meals in the hall to see 'how mannerly they eat and drink, and to their communication and other forms of court'.[17] The courtesy books often tell a young gentleman not only how to eat politely but how to perform the various household offices expected in a large household. John Russell's *Book of Nurture* and *Book of Courtesy* are good examples.

The later courtesy books show a different world. Francis Seager's *School of Virtue*, which was written in the mid-sixteenth century, concentrates on teaching the child who is serving its parents in its own home, rather than living in a great household. This is a reflection of the fact that middle-class families, whose children went to school and lived at home rather than being sent into other households, now aspired to learn good manners. It is also a reflection of the changes in society. The big ecclesiastical households, where previously many of the children had been educated, had been dissolved and it was becoming more common even for wealthy children to be brought up at home, and later to be sent to the universities.

Hunting was the favourite sport of the aristocracy. Game was far more prestigious than farmed meat. This picture shows deer hunting in the background and hawking in the foreground. (Samantha Doty)

As dining became more private, the importance of certain rituals and certain items of plate declined. The elaborate ceremony described by John Russell for serving dinner to a lord only really made sense when the lord was dining in the hall. The ceremonial salt cellar was another item that had significance only when the lord dined in hall. At a private dinner it would do little more than take up space on the table, so that the importance of salts gradually declined from the end of the sixteenth century.

This is not to say that, in the grandest circles at least, dining had now become completely informal. A German visitor to Queen Elizabeth's Court described in some detail how her meals were served, including the fact that 'twelve trumpets and two kettle drums made the hall ring for half an hour together' to announce the fact that Her Majesty was dining. There was much ceremony, including an elaborate tasting for poison, but while this was all very public the queen's meals were very private indeed. 'The Queen sups and dines alone with very few attendants, and it is very seldom that any body, foreigner or native, is admitted at that time and then only at the intercession of somebody in power,' the German visitor went on to say. The ceremony was public, to remind people of the power of the queen, but Her Majesty preferred the convenience of dining alone in peace and quiet.[18]

Changes in dining habits are also reflected in the cookery books of the time. As private dining became the rule, the way in which the table was laid modified. As everyone was now sitting around the same table it became important that the dishes were laid out as attractively as possible. Cookery books began not only to provide recipes, but also to give suggested table plans showing how best to arrange the dishes. Gervais Markham in *The English Housewife*, first published in 1615, describes the importance of knowing how to seat guests according to precedence, and also of how to serve up the dishes: 'For what avails it our good housewife to be never so skilful in the parts of cookery, is she want skill to marshal the dishes, and set every one in his due place, giving precedency according to fashion and custom; it is like to a fencer leading a band of men in a rout, who knows the use of the weapon, but not how to put the men in order.'[19] He then goes on to describe when to serve the various dishes and how to lay them all out on the table. The dishes would be displayed in a symmetrical pattern (see how the dishes are laid out in the picture of Sir Nicholas Unton dining, on page 106). By the late seventeenth century the table designs shown in cookery books became very complicated indeed and laying the table had become almost an art form in itself.

These, then were the basics of the serving and eating of food in the sixteenth century. Good table manners were essential if you wished to move in higher circles, and as a reminder of this here are some words from Seager's *School of Virtue*, in wonderfully bad verse:

> Of good manners learn so much as thou can;
> It will thee prefer when thou are a man.
> Aristotle, the philosopher, this worthy saying writ,
> That manners in a child are more requisite
> Than playing on instruments and other vain pleasure;
> For virtuous manners is a most precious treasure.[20]

CHAPTER NINE

Feasts, Entertainments and Luxury Food

Feasting and entertainments are important to all societies, and the Tudors certainly knew how to enjoy them. At one level there were the feasts that were enjoyed by all classes of society, such as Shrovetide and Christmas. In court circles, though, entertainments were useful tools for the Tudor monarchs, allowing them to put across certain messages to both their own subjects and to foreign countries.

The greatest of the feasts celebrated was Christmas. This, of course, covered twelve days, but unlike the modern Christmas the celebrations did not begin until Christmas Day itself. Advent was mostly a time of fasting, and as Advent only ended after mass on Christmas Day, the festivities could not begin before then. The two most celebrated days of Christmas were New Year and the final day of celebration, Twelfth Night.

There is already a large number of books written about the history of Christmas so I will not go into great detail here. There was, though, a definite purpose to the Tudor Christmas. At a time when society was very strictly organized, Christmas acted as a kind of pressure-release valve, a time when everything was turned on its head.

There were different days when certain sections of society were allowed an unusal degree of freedom. Children, for example, had their day on 6 December, St Nicholas's day. St Nicholas had a particular association with children because he saved three poor girls from becoming prostitutes by providing them with dowries, and also because he brought back to life three little boys who had been dismembered.[1]

Christmas, then as now, had a variety of dishes associated with it. The first was the boar's head, which formed the centrepiece of the Christmas Day meal. It was garnished with rosemary and bay and evidently was presented to the diners with some style, as told by the many boar's head carols which still exist. Here is a verse from one such carol, found in Richard Hill's commonplace book compiled between about 1500 and 1534:

> The bores hede in ondes I bringe,
> With garlondes day and birdes singinge.
> I pray you all, helpe me to singe,
> Qui estis in convivio [Those who are present].[2]

Thomas Tusser in *Five Hundred Points of Good Husbandry* suggests a number of dishes that, lower down society, the housewife should provide for her guests at Christmas. He mentions mutton, pork, veal, souse (pickled pig's feet and ears), brawn, cheese and apples, although none of these items was connected especially with Christmas; they were all associated with feasting generally. He also talks of serving turkey, but only as part of a list of other luxurious items that the housewife should provide. It does not seem to be the centrepiece in the way that the boar's head was in grander circles.[3]

One important item associated with Twelfth Night was the Twelfth cake. This was a fruitcake into which an object or objects might be baked. These might be a coin, or coins, or a dried bean and pea. The idea was that whoever found the item in their piece of cake became the King of the Bean or Queen of the Pea. They would then become host and hostess for the evening's entertainments. This tradition is still maintained in France, where a gold ring or even a gold figure of the Christ child is baked into an almond tart.[4]

As the King of the Bean was expected to entertain everybody, often his choice was not left to chance in grander circles. Payments and gifts made to the 'King of the Bene' at both the Scots and English Courts suggest that in large households, at least, often someone was actually appointed to the position.[5]

The exact nature of the cake, despite it being such an important part of Twelfth Night, remains something of a mystery. Very likely it contained dried fruit, but the earliest evidence comes from a tract printed in Geneva in 1620 which lists the main ingredients as flour, honey, ginger and pepper.[6]

The Royal Household, being in some ways a household just like any other, celebrated along with the rest of the country. However, the Royal Household was in an odd position. Entertainments there would be seen by all the most important members of English society, together with visitors and ambassadors from foreign powers. They provided an ideal opportunity for reminding everyone of the power of the monarch. Sometimes the most innocent of occasions could be turned to political ends, like the ceremonies surrounding Twelfth Night. In 1564 the English ambassador to the Scots Court, Thomas Randolph, sent a description of the festivities at the Court of Mary, Queen of Scots, to Lord Robert Dudley, the great favourite of Elizabeth I. 'The Queen of the Bean was Mary Fleming, one of Her Majesty's maids of honour, who 'was in a gowne of cloath of silver; her head, her neck, her shoulders, the rest of her whole body, so besett with stones, that more in our whole jewell house wer not to be found. The Queen herself [was] apparelled in colour whyt and black, [no] jewell or gold about her, bot the ring that I brought from the Queen's Majestie hanging at her breast, with a lace of whyte and black about her neck'.[7] Queen Mary would, of course, have been aware of the English ambassador's presence, and the whole scene would have been stage-managed. Allowing centre-stage to a maid of honour was a way of demonstrating to Elizabeth that Mary was so secure in her position that she could allow herself to be 'upstaged' by one of her attendants. The fact that the only jewel she herself chose to wear was Queen Elizabeth's ring cannot have been an accident.

Another tradition associated with Christmas was that of wassailing. This was the remains of old fertility rites, when a toast would be drunk to fruit trees in the hope of making them produce a good crop in the following year. Whatever its origins, it was certainly an opportunity for plenty of drinking. There was no one traditional wassail cup for the whole country as every region had its own particular tradition. The wassail cup might be of cider, ale, or some spiced ale such as lambswool, a kind of spiced beer which was served warm.

Wassailing was a part of Christmas for everyone, from the highest to the lowest. Even at Court the tradition was maintained. Here is a description of Henry VII's wassail, from the Household Ordinances of 1494:

Item as for the voide on twelfth day at night, the King and Queene ought to take it in the halle, and as for the wassell, the Steward and the treasurer shall come forward with their staves in their hands, the King's swere and the Queen's next, with their towells about their necks, and noe man beare noe dishes but such as bee sworne for the mouthe, especially such as the kinge shall eat of . . .

Item the chappell to stand on the one side of the hall, and when the Steward cometh in at the hall doore with the wassell, he must crie three tymes, wassell, wassell, wassell and then the chappell to answere with a good songe . . .[8]

This strict etiquette must have made Henry VII's wassail a vastly more formal occasion than the one his subjects enjoyed.

Christmas was not the only time of year associated with certain types of food. May Day was another great celebration. It was a day that Henry VIII celebrated with style. In *The Triumphant Reigne of Kyng Henry the VIII* Edward Hall records one occasion on which the royal party was met by 'Robin Hood and his Merry Men' while out maying, and was entertained to a feast by them in a leafy bower in the woods. Henry's subjects also celebrated with enthusiasm. John Stow talks of the citizens of London 'going into the Woods and Meadows to divert themselves'.[9] It was a day associated with fertility rites so the games in the woods were not necessarily innocent, although more blameless community sports and dancing were also usual. In any case, the revellers would be welcomed home with cakes and cream.[10] Cream was a great luxury for ordinary people as most of it was needed to make butter and cheese, both essential parts of the diet in the sixteenth century.

Certain festivals were celebrated by certain sections of society. Thomas Tusser includes a list of feast days kept by farm labourers, advising 'Good huswives, whom God hath enriched ynough/forget not the feasts that belong to the plough.' The first of these was Plough Monday, the first Monday after Twelfth Night. This was seen as the start of the agricultural year. The next day to be celebrated was a general festival, Shrovetide, or Shrove Tuesday, when fritters and pancakes were the order of the day.

Tusser goes on to describe a few regional festivals. In Northamptonshire sheep shearing was an occasion for a feast which included 'wafers and cakes'. Wafers were thin, crisp cakes baked in an iron, rather like modern-day waffles, only somewhat thinner. Considering the importance of wool to the English economy it seems strange that this was perhaps only a regional feast. Sheep shearing must have been celebrated throughout the country.

In Essex and Suffolk the end of the wheat sowing was celebrated with seed cake, pastries and 'furmentie'. The latter was made of wheat boiled with milk and seasoned with spices. In grander circles it had been served with venison since the Middle Ages.[11] A general celebration throughout the country was the harvest home supper. Tusser mentions goose as the traditional dish.

He finishes his list of celebrations with a reminder of the importance of feeding the household staff well:

> Good ploughman looke weekly, of custome and right
> for roast meete on Sundaies and Thursdaies at night

> This dooing and keeping such custome and guise
> they call thee good huswife, they love thee likewise.[12]

Tusser's audience, although not the very top of society, would still have been in about the top 10 or 15 per cent in the Tudor hierarchy, and so could have afforded to feed its staff with roast meat twice a week.

Advent and Lent were other occasions when special food was eaten, but as times of fast rather than feast. The Lent fast in particular was really born of necessity. Late spring was the time when the last year's store of food would have been running low, and so limiting its use was sensible. Thomas Tusser acknowledges this fact in another one of his rhymes:

> A plot set downe, for fermers quiet
> as time requires, to frame his diet:
> With sometimes fish and sometimes fast.
> that household store may longer last.[13]

For the wealthy, Lent was a time of fasting but in relative terms. Meat, milk and eggs might be forbidden but over the centuries cooks had found ways of coping with this. Recipe books of the time are full of ways of providing luxurious meals despite the restrictions. Milk could be replaced with almond milk, made from ground almonds mixed with anything from white wine to fish broth.[14] A variety of luxurious fish dishes replaced the meat dishes. A sample menu for a fish day at Henry VIII and Katherine of Aragon's table includes plaice, porpoise or seal, salmon, pike, eels or lampreys, carp, trout, crab, lobster and sea bream.[15]

All Fridays and Saturdays were also fast days, although the restrictions were more relaxed than they were during Lent. On ordinary Fridays outside Lent it seems to have been only meat that was not allowed. The more important members of Henry VIII's Court were provided with eggs and butter on both days, just as they were on other days of the week.[16] Tusser states that there were three fast days in a week, Friday, Saturday and Wednesday,[17] but at Court Wednesday was definitely a meat day. Possibly, for the less affluent, observing the fast on an extra day a week was one way of making meat supplies go further.

The people who must have enjoyed fish days least would have been those who had to eat stockfish. This was dried fish which was rock hard and had to be beaten with a wooden hammer and soaked in warm water for two hours before it could be eaten. Fresh fish, unless you lived by the sea, was a luxury and often it was bought only for the master and his family in a large household. Everyone else had to make do with stockfish. It was sometimes eaten by grander people, as the Goodwife of Paris gives a recipe for making it into rissoles. The rissoles were made by mincing up the stockfish with chestnuts and skirret roots, skirrets being a species of water parsnip. They were also expensively flavoured with spices and sugar.[18]

Besides the food associated with certain occasions there was luxury food which was served whenever it could be obtained and which was intended to delight and impress. One such food was fruit. A better-off person's meal in the sixteenth century finished with fruit. Cavendish describes Cardinal Wolsey as being 'not fully dined but being at his fruits' when the Earl of Northumberland came to arrest him.[19] Henry VIII's meals also ended with fruit, although exactly what fruit is not specified apart from the fact that oranges and pippins (a variety of apples) are often included in the menu.[20] Ordinary people could also enjoy the fruit they grew in their gardens, but imported luxuries like oranges were far beyond their means. At Court only the grander courtiers had a service of fruit as part of their meals. The lower courtiers, such as the king's yeomen of the guard, were not so lucky. This was probably because the fruit was usually preserved in sugar, which was too expensive to lavish on the less important members of the Royal Household.

However it was served, the variety of fruit to choose from was increasing. As fruit was part of the royal diet, Henry VIII wanted the best for his table. In 1533 Richard Harris, the royal fruiterer, brought over various grafts from the Low Countries and France to improve the royal stocks, and a kind of model fruit nursery seems to have been set up at Tenham in Kent. William Lambarde, in his *Perambulation of Kent*, describes Harris's work as follows: 'our honest patriote, Richard Harrys . . . planted by his great coste and rare industrie the sweete Cherry, the temperate Pipyn and the golden Renate. For this man seeing that this Realme (which wanteth neither the favour of the sunne nor the fat of the Soile, meete for the making of good apples) was nevertheless served chiefly with fruit from foreign Regions abroad. . . .'[21]

The development of the Kent market gardens was helped by the politics of the time. The Low Countries were a source of fruit-growing expertise, which is why many of Harris's grafts came from there. The religious wars of the sixteenth century caused many Walloon refugees to come to England from the Low Countries, and many of them settled in Kent and set up market gardens.[22]

The building of the magnificent new palace of Nonsuch was another stimulus to English fruit growing. Henry VIII had new varieties of fruit introduced to ensure that the gardens were as superb as the palace itself. One of the new varieties was the apricot, described by Turner in his *Herbal* of 1548: 'Some englishe me cal the fruite an Abricock. Me thynkesing that we have very fewe of these trees as yet, it were better to cal it, an hasty Peche tree because it is lyke a peche and it is a great whyle rype before the peche trees wherefore the fruite of thes tree is called malum precox.'[23]

Thomas Tusser, in *Five Hundred Points of Household Husbandry*, lists a wide range of fruits: grapes, strawberries, crab apples, barberries, raspberries, gooseberries, apples, apricots, bullices, cherries, plums, damsons, filiberts, medlars, whortleberries, mulberries, peaches, pears and quinces. (The crab apples, incidentally, were intended not for eating, but for making verjuice which was used for preserving and in cooking.) The book is aimed at the less-well-off housewife (although not at those at the very bottom of society by any means) and it would be surprising if such people were growing much in the way of grapes. As discussed in the section on wine, it was difficult to get them to ripen in England.

It was precisely the fact that more delicate fruits were difficult and expensive to grow which made them so desirable. After all, fruit such as apples and pears were available to everyone, so they were not much of a status symbol. Serving your guests with one of the new varieties of peach or apricot, which as yet might not be widely grown in England, was much more the thing to do.

The eating of fruit was not always encouraged by the health manuals of the day, but then neither was it always condemned. In *Castel of Helth* Sir Thomas Elyot considered that 'all fruites generally are noyfull to manne and do ingender yll humours'.[24] He did believe that at one time mankind had lived on fruit, but since we had learned to grow corn and to eat fish and vegetables our constitutions had changed, so that now it was no longer such a good idea.

Plum stones found on the wreck of the *Mary Rose*. (Mary Rose Trust no. 86.0045)

Elyot does not, though, condemn the eating of fruit out of hand, and even recommends eating it after meals. Apples consumed after meals 'are right holsome and do confirme the stomacke and make good digestion, specially if they be rosted or baken'. Generally he advocates eating cooked, rather than raw, fruit and also often recommends eating sugar and fruit together. Sugar was thought to aid the digestion while fruit was considered hard to digest, so this advice seemed to make sense.

It is heartening to know that the experts could not agree even in Tudor times. Andrew Boorde, in *Dyetary of Health*, is more positive about fruit, although like Elyot he often recommends eating it with sugar. Some fruit was good raw, however. 'Grapes, swete and newe, be nutrytyne and doth stimulat the flesshe.'[25]

Acceptance of fruit seems to have grown wider with time. In *Paradisi in Sole*, a gardening book first published in 1620, John Parkinson comments that 'those peaches that are very moist and waterish (as many of them are) doo soone putrifie in the stomach' but concludes by saying that peaches are 'much and often well accepted with all the Gentry of the Kingdome'.[26]

As fresh fruit was not always available large quantities of it were preserved in various forms. Housewifery manuals are full of recipes for doing so. Markham, for example, lists several ways of preserving quinces, including one in which they are placed whole into cider, one in which a kind of quince purée is preserved and another in which they are preserved as a kind of sweetmeat.[27]

Though a wealthy person's diet was based on meat, as we have already seen certain vegetables did reach the grandest tables. There must have been an interest in them among the well-to-do as

The aim of the Renaissance gardener was to create paradise on earth, hence the
choice of subject matter for the title page of John Parkinson's gardening book
Paradisi in Sole. (Guildhall Library, Corporation of London)

gardening books of the time go into some detail about how to grow them. Thomas Hill's *Gardener's Labyrinth* (first published in 1577) gives detailed advice about growing a whole range of them. The 1580 edition of *Five Hundred Points of Good Husbandry*, catering for a slightly less affluent market than Hill, also mentions a surprisingly large range of herbs and vegetables to grow for use in 'sallets and sauce', including sea holly, skirrets, endives, cucumbers and rocket. Among the 'herbes and rootes to boile or to butter' are beans, cabbage, carrots, citrons (long, pear-shaped fruit with a thick, yellow rind, still used today as the basis for candied peel), gourds, navewes (a kind of rape), pumpkins, parsnips, runcivall pease (marrowfat peas), rape (turnip) and turneps (presumably a different kind of turnip to the rape). The range in John Parkinson's book is even wider. Clearly interest in vegetables was growing.

Towards the end of the sixteenth century cookery books also started to make much more mention of vegetables. The fashion for eating sallats, as discussed in the introduction, was one reason for this interest, but not all vegetables were eaten as part of a sallat. The 1633 edition of Gerard's *Herball* talks of several vegetables being highly prized. For example, the 'middle pulpe' of globe artichokes is said to be eaten 'both raw with pepper and salt, and commonly boyled with the broth of fat flesh, with pepper added, and [is] accounted a dainty dish' especially as it procures 'bodily lust'. The middle leaves, too, were cherished, being 'brought to the table as a great service together with other junkets; they are eaten with pepper and salt as be the raw Artichokes'.[28] However, John Parkinson states that Jerusalem artichokes, which he calls 'Canada potatoes', have become so common that 'even the most vulgar begin to despise them, whereas they were first among us, they were dainties for a Queene'.[29] The growth of the city of London over the period, together with the increased interest in fruit and vegetables, led to the founding in 1605 of both a Gardener's and a Fruiterer's Company.[30]

At this stage it is worth mentioning the potato, as it is the most famous of the vegetables introduced into England at the time. In the 1633 edition of *Herball* two types of potato are included. One is called the 'potatus' or 'potatoes', which is a sweet potato and is referred to by John Parkinson as a Spanish potato.[31] Gerard found that when he tried to grow the plant in his garden it rotted once winter came. He describes this type as 'common and ordinarie meate' to the Spaniards, Italians and Indians and says that a conserve made from it is 'no lesse toothsome, wholesome and dainty than of the

Plate from John Parkinson's *Paradisi in Sole* showing the types of potato. The 'Spanish Potato' or sweet potato is number 2, top right, the 'Virginia Potato' (the one we call the potato) is number 3, bottom left, and the Potato of Canada or Jerusalem Artichoke is number 4, bottom right. (Guildhall Library, Corporation of London)

flesh of Quinces', which was high praise indeed. Quince preserves were greatly prized at the time.

The other variety is the 'Virginia potato', which is the one familiar to us today. Gerard describes it as being like the sweet potato, 'a food, as also meate for pleasure, equall in goodnesse and wholesomenesse unto the same, being either rosted in the embers or boyled and eated with oyle, vinegar, and pepper or dressed any other way by the hand of some cunning in cookerie'.[32] Parkinson also praises it highly.[33]

The way that both types of potato are described implies that they are unusual delicacies, and indeed potatoes were not to become the common food of ordinary people until the eighteenth century. John Parkinson clearly regards them as a luxury as he comments that 'they are used to be baked with Marrow, Sugar, Spice and other things in Pyes, which are a dainty and costly dish for the table. The Comfit makers preserve them, and candy them as divers other things and so ordered is very delicate, fit to accompany other banquetting dishes . . .'. He is talking of the sweet potato in this instance, but adds that 'the Virginia potato being ordered after all these waies before specified maketh almost as delicate meate as the former'.

The use of the potato in conserves sounds very odd today but made perfect sense at the time. Wealthier people's meals in the Middle Ages often ended with a compost, which was a dish of root vegetables and fruit, such as pears, mixed up in kind of sweet and sour sauce. So the idea of putting root vegetables in sugar was a very old one.

The tomato was another famous new introduction of the time, though again it was not commonly eaten until much later, probably in the nineteenth century. Opinion was still divided as to whether or not it was safe to eat but Markham talks of sowing tomato seeds in the garden in March.[34] It was known as the 'apple of love' as, like many new and curious items, it was considered an aphrodisiac. Gerard refers to it as both the 'Apple of Love' and the 'Golden Apple'. He says that the Spanish ate them 'prepared and boiled with pepper, salt, and oile' and also with 'oile, vinegar and pepper mixed together for sauce to their meat, even as we in these cold Countries doe Mustard'. Even so, Gerard considers that they 'yeeld very little nourishment to the bodie, and the same nought and corrupt'.[35]

The very seasonal nature of the food supply in Tudor times meant that for all classes of society diets changed with the seasons. Even the very rich could not have delicacies such as fresh strawberries in

January or fresh cherries in March as it is perfectly possible to do today. This was also true of certain types of meat and poultry. *A Proper New Booke of Cokerye* published in the mid-sixteenth century (probably in 1545), opens with advice as to what is in season when. Here is a sample:

> Beife and Bacon is good at all tymes in the yere. Mutton is good at all tymes, but from Easter to my Sommer is worste. A fatte pygge is ever in season. A goose is worste in midsomer mone and best in stubble tyme, but when they be yong grene geese, then they be beste. Veale is beste in Januarye, and February, and all other times good. Lambe and yonge kydde is beste between Christmas and lente, and good from Easter to Witsontyde . . .

Similarly Tusser lists the appropriate time for certain foods. For example, Easter was the time to eat veal and bacon and Michaelmas (29 September) the time to eat fresh herrings and also 'fatted crones', the old female sheep who were past their prime and ready for the pot. Christmas was the only time when it was right to 'play and make good cheere' with a clear conscience and enjoy the best of food that you had. The rest of the year you always had to make the most of what was in season, keeping in mind future supplies of food.

The lavishness of the royal table was a matter of politics. As we have seen, the Tudors liked to make the point that they could afford to do things in style. It was the same when the more important nobility entertained the monarch. It was a very good idea to display your loyalty by sparing no expense. The kind of food served on these occasions would be a range of all that was most expensive, and served in great profusion. Heavily spiced sauces, intricate sugarwork[36] and luxury meats like venison and gamebirds would appear on the table, all elaborately served to demonstrate the skill of the cooks and the deep pockets of the host. Cardinal Wolsey was a man who was very much aware of this.

In *Life and Death of Cardinal Wolsey* George Cavendish describes at some length an entertainment given by the cardinal for Henry VIII. At first the king is not even there, until it seems that the day of feasting and entertainments is almost over. Some 'foreign visitors' then arrive by water, announced by much firing of cannon 'which made such a rumble in the air that it was like thunder'. These visitors were, of course, Henry and his gentlemen in disguise. The cardinal had to guess which one was the king, and to everyone's amusement he guessed wrongly, choosing instead Sir Edward Neville, who apparently looked very like Henry. The feasting, to everyone's surprise, started all over again, with a complete new set of dishes being served.

The lavish nature of the entertainment is described lovingly by Cavendish, who depicts the 'sweetly perfumed cloths' for the tables and the vast number of dishes – 'two hundred . . . or above of wonderous costly meats and devices, subtly devised'. This was just the *second* banquet. It was important on such occasions that the host should give the impression that money was no object at all. The cardinal evidently succeeded and provided entertainment that was 'to the great comfort of the King and pleasant regard of the nobility there assembled'.

The political importance of such entertainments was not lost on Cavendish. This is his comment on Wolsey's efforts to entertain his sovereign: 'It delighted him so much to have the King's pleasant princely presence, that nothing was to him more delectable than to cheer his sovereign lord, to whom he owed so much obedience and loyalty – as reason required no less, all things considered.'[37] Elizabeth's subjects, too, were to realize that no expense was too great if it meant that you kept the royal favour.

Elizabeth's famous progresses were also highly political. They are often dismissed as a clever way of making courtiers foot the bill for feeding and entertaining the Court, but they were far more than that. Since the Middle Ages kings had lived on the move, not only to check up on what was happening in the various regions of their realm but also to show themselves off. They were well aware of how much a personal visit from the king could boost their popularity – or at least bring home the fact that the sovereign was a force to be reckoned with. Even now, though the media brings the faces of politicians into our homes every day, the politicians themselves certainly recognize the importance of the personal visit, especially at election time. Elizabeth was not one to miss such a good opportunity.

Those who entertained Elizabeth were acutely aware of the political weight of a visit from her, and the festivities they organized carefully reflected this. A visit to Sudeley Castle in 1592 coincided with her birthday, 7 September. The masque offered for her entertainment flattered her suitably, describing her as she 'by whome all the shepheards should have their flocks in safety, and their own lives, all the country quietnes, and the whole world astonishment'.[38]

Just in case this were not precaution enough, the 'shepherds' knelt at the end of the show to apologize, as they had also dared to play the part of kings and queens in her presence.

At a great court entertainment it was as well not to be so overwhelmed by the magnificent food and drink that you forgot everything else. Meals on these occasions were only part of the festivities. The profusion of food and the wonderful dishes on which it was served were part of a carefully stage-managed entertainment. These entertainments were intended not only to delight and impress but also to convey political messages. Everything might have significance, from the clothes people wore to the gifts they exchanged.

The most famous piece of pagentry of Henry VIII's reign was the Field of Cloth of Gold, which took place in 1520. This was a meeting between Henry and the French king, Francis I, which lasted just over two weeks.[39] It was the most magnificent spectacle imaginable, as Henry even had a temporary palace built for the occasion. The place had stone foundations and real glass windows, although the walls were wooden and the roof was made of oilcloth. It was absolutely huge – the walls were about 30 ft high – and came with a complete set of offices, such as cellars, a pitcher house and a ewery, just like a permanent palace.[40]

The event was supposed to be a kind of summit meeting to discuss the Treaty of Perpetual Friendship that had been signed by the two countries back in 1518. It became a kind of struggle between the two kings, who were great personal rivals. The whole event grew in size until finally each king was being attended by about six thousand people. The logistics involved in feeding and housing that number of people in an area where there were no large towns were incredible, but behind the logistics lay a political struggle: which king was the more powerful?

The importance of each king's display of wealth and therefore power was not lost on those attending the event. The ambassadors' reports from the Field carefully record every detail – gifts exchanged, the horses that people were riding and even the clothes worn. The ambassadors knew that everything could have a hidden meaning and they made sure that they recorded every detail so as to miss none of the messages the two kings intended the rest of Europe to hear. For example, Soardino, the Mantuan ambassador at the Court of France, reported to his master, the Marquis of Mantua, that Francis I had better horses than Henry (though he was hardly unbiased). The horse

Tudor tournaments were complicated affairs. Among other equipment, a knight was supposed to have an impresa, which was a picture and a motto which would put across personal intentions, ambition or feelings. Here are some Elizabethan examples. (College of Arms, MS M6, ff. 56v and 57)

he particularly praised came from Mantua and was known as Dappled Duke. It was given to Henry by King Francis. The horse Henry gave in exchange, a Neopolitan courser, was considered by Soardino to be greatly inferior.[41] Horses were a significant gift because they were the usual mode of transport for the wealthy, as well as being used in battle.

The costumes worn were also recorded in great detail as sometimes they had a political significance which to us would seem almost unbelievable. The Tudors used a great deal of symbolism, and in the sixteenth century a king's clothing could signify anything from a declaration of love to a threat of war.

Naturally a tournament formed part of the entertainments. By the sixteenth century tournaments were basically an occasion for a very elaborate display of wealth. They also gave the aristocracy the chance to show off their military skills, but the aim was most definitely not to kill the opponent. Tournaments could still be dangerous and deaths did occur from time to time. Sir James Parker, for example, was killed in a tournament held in 1492 and the French king Henri II died in the same way in 1559 – but these were unfortunate accidents.

The amount of pageantry was breathtaking. The contenders in a tournament came in amazing disguises, which were all made of the finest materials like costly silk velvets and real cloth of gold. Often their clothing was designed to have a meaning. Edward Hall describes one costume which Henry wore at the Field. It was decorated with 'waves of water worrke, and every wave wrought and frised with Damaske golde, this woorke was laied lose on russet velvet and knitte together with poyntes of golde, which waves signified the Lordshippe of the narrow sea'. The 'Narrow Sea' was the Tudors' name for the English Channel, so Henry was warning Francis of his military intentions.[42]

The problem with symbolism is that it can easily get over-complicated and the meaning then becomes lost. This seems to have been a particular problem at the Field of Cloth of Gold, where everyone was looking for meaning in everything. Even those well used to the complexities of court life began to get confused. Francis wore a series of costumes for the tournament which seemed to tell a story of courtly love, of his heart being in endless pain when his lady did not respond to his affections. Hall provides a careful description of these costumes, together with an explanation of the message he thinks was intended, but concludes with the despairing comment that 'this was the interpretacion made, but whether it were so in all thinges or not I may not saye'.[43]

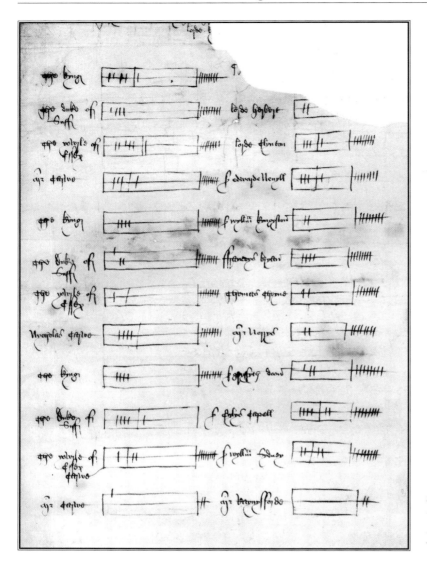

Score cheque from a tournament held at Greenwich in 1516 (College of Arms, Tournament cheque lc)

Another important part of court entertainments in the sixteenth century was the distribution of gifts to show off the wealth and generosity of the monarch. At one entertainment early in Henry's reign, in 1511, the king wore a costume decorated with gold ornaments. He then arranged for some of these decorations to be given to the Spanish ambassadors who had asked for them 'for in the beginning they thought that they had been counterfait, and not of golde'. What better way of showing off the king's wealth than by making such a gift? The problem was that on this occasion things went rather wrong. The arrangement was that at an agreed time the ambassadors would be allowed to pull some of the decorations off the king's clothing. Various onlookers saw this and decided that it was a general invitation to join in. Both the king and Sir Thomas Knyvet found themselves stripped of their clothing, even down to their doublets and hose. The bestowing of such gifts was too important a part of the display to be stopped as a result, but from then on it was carried out more carefully.[44]

The scale and importance of court festivities in the sixteenth century is evident from the increasingly complicated bureaucracy which developed for organizing them. During the reign of Henry VII court entertainments were planned and organized by the king and the council, the body of men which advised him. Other entertainments might be arranged by different people, as the need arose. By the time of Henry VIII, though, things were changing. Court entertainments became larger and more complicated as increasing numbers of people began to get involved, from artists and craftsmen who designed and made sets and costumes to the labourers who would transport and erect the various bits of scenery. All these people had to be supervised, so that soon a Master of Revels was needed. At first the master was appointed for a specific period to deal with a certain set of entertainments and then he returned to his ordinary job, but by the end of Henry VIII's reign things had grown too complicated for this arrangement. In 1545, almost at the end of the king's reign, the title was conferred by patent for life.[45]

Revels were held in the short reigns of Edward and Mary, but neither ruled for long enough to stamp his or her character on them. Other factors which could not have helped were the political uncertainties of their reigns and, for Mary, the uncomfortable atmosphere at Court created by her exceedingly unpopular marriage to Philip of Spain. Under Elizabeth, however, court entertainments took a new direction.

Elizabeth was in an enormously difficult situation. The religious divide between the old Catholic order and the new Protestant one was by this time pulling most of continental Europe apart and England was far from being free of these tensions. There were other pressures, too, causing disunity within the nation. The merchant classes in the towns were flourishing, while many of the people at the bottom of society were struggling to survive and sometimes were even being forced to wander around the country looking for work. The old aristocracy found they could no longer maintain the large

households they had been used to, and were being overshadowed by 'newcomer' families. Elizabeth realized that something had to be done to hold the nation together. Her response was to turn herself into a kind of cult, which explains on the one hand the large number of symbolic portraits of her which still exist, and on the other hand the very elaborate court festivities such as her progresses.[46]

The fame of the Tudor court entertainments should not mislead us into imagining that even the grandest people lived in a constant social whirl of tournaments and feasting. Lavish entertainments like the Field of Cloth of Gold or the entertainments provided for Elizabeth at Sudeley Castle were exceptional, even in court circles. The huge feasts with hundreds of dishes such as Cardinal Wolsey served to Henry VIII were hardly the typical daily diet even for the very grand. In noble households the everyday fare even for the master and mistress of the house was not necessarily lavish. The Northumberland household accounts show that the earl and his lady and their guests ate certain foods only at times of celebration. Here is one example concerning plovers: 'Item it is thought good that no PLUVERS be bought at noo season bot oonely in Chrysteynmas and princypall Feasts and my Lode to be seryde therewith and his Boorde-end and non other and to be boght for j*d* a piece or j*d* ob at most.'[47]

This is part of a long list of items which were to be bought only at certain times and only when the price was within a certain limit. Great lords could all put on lavish displays when it was expected of them, such as at Christmas, but this was only possible if strict economy was maintained at other times, otherwise they were liable to bankrupt themselves. Huge banquets were very different from the everyday diet even in the highest circles.

CHAPTER TEN

Banquets

In the sixteenth century the word 'banquet' had two meanings. The first was the one we still use today, that is, a grand meal. The second was rather different. It meant a dessert course consisting of various luxurious foods, often eaten in a specially constructed banqueting house.

The idea of the dessert course banquet had developed from feasts held by the wealthy and important in the Middle Ages. Often the top table at a feast was served with spiced wine, wafers and various spices at the end of a meal to aid digestion, and so as to finish on a suitably luxurious note. At this stage the hall would be in the process of being cleared of the trestle tables used for dining, so it made sense to go into another, more comfortable room for this course. Thus began the tradition of eating what later became the dessert course in a different room, together with the tradition that it was only served to a small selection of the grander guests, rather than to everyone who had been invited to the feast.[1]

There was an additional reason for withdrawing to another room. The servants had to eat and the hall was the only room in which there would be space for them to do so. This was permitted because in the sixteenth century servants were not seen as inferior, as they were in the eighteenth and nineteenth centuries. In large households especially, some very well-bred young men might be involved in serving dinner and it would have seemed reasonable for the guests to wait for their spices until these men had eaten.

In France this section of the meal became known as 'the void'. It was served with great ceremony, involving processions of household officials bearing impressive cups and spice plates. A simpler version of this elaborate ceremony even seeped down to the middle classes. The *Goodwife of Paris* describes how, at the end of a grand meal, hippocras and wafers were served, and then everyone's hands were ceremonially washed. Grace was said and then everyone stood and went to another room to allow the servants to sit down and eat. Once the servants had finished, they served the company with wine and spices, after which it was time for the guests to leave.[2]

This fashion had evidently come to England by Henry VII's time, as his Household Ordinances of 1494 give a detailed account of what should happen on 'the even of the day when a voide shall be had'. Clearly it would be quite an elaborate occasion and seems not to have taken place very regularly as the ordinances suggest that it happened only when the king decided that it should.

The ordinances remind the usher of his duties: to warn the spicery to prepare the spice plates, the cellar to have the wine and the cups ready, and to warn 'the King's sewers and esquires which must waite that tyme'. The sewers and esquires were the waiting staff who would be expected to attend in large numbers to add to the magnificence of the occasion.

These ordinances cover every detail, even the fact that there must be sufficient lights fot the occasion. The void was a reflection of the king's power and status. A great mass of expensive wax candles lighting the event would have added to the sense of overwhelming luxury.[3]

These instructions were important. The void was intended to impress and the elaborate ceremony was another way of reminding everyone of their social position. It was also an occasion on which the king might choose to honour someone by handing them his cup and spice plate after he had been served, and of course it was yet another occasion on which the wealth and power of a grand household could be displayed. Edward Hall describes an amazing void held to impress the French ambassadors in 1527, which included the use of 'lx spice plates of silver and gilt as great as men with ease might beare'.[4]

As the sixteenth century progressed the void became a totally separate part of the meal, developing into a banquet itself. Banquets became far more than just a form of entertainment. They became very much an expression of sophisticated tastes and behaviour.

A banquet, whether small and intimate or large scale, was supposed to be a delight to the senses at all levels. The best of food and wine would be served, and enormous effort was made to ensure that it was served in a way that was a delight to the eye as much as to the palette. The venue was designed to be as original and beautiful as possible, with all sorts of architectural and even horticultural novelties being called into service to please the guests.

The banqueting hall at Melford Hall, Suffolk. The panelling is original, showing how comfortable life was becoming for the wealthy. (National Trust Photographic Library/Martin Charles)

The small, intimate banquet was also supposed to be an occasion when the guests could show off their elegant manners. It provided an opportunity to demonstrate your skills in the art of conversation, something much prized in Elizabethan England, and you might even have a chance to show off your skills in music and poetry too.

Banqueting houses could be the most fantastic of places. Some of them were only temporary, although that did not stop them being almost unbelievably magnificent. The French encampment at the Field of Cloth of Gold incorporated a banqueting pavilion. It had foundations of brick a foot high and the wooden walls, which were 30 feet high, were painted to look like brick. Built in the form of a rotunda, according to one account it had a circumference of 240 paces.[5] It was covered with azure velvet powdered with fleur-de-lis and was hung inside with tapestry.[6]

Henry VIII's encampment at the Field was to have included a banqueting house but unfortunately there was no time to build it. On 10 April, about two months before the event, the commissioners warned that there were not enough resources to finish both the chapel and the banqueting house, and so only the chapel was finished.[7]

One of the most magnificent banqueting houses was the one built at Greenwich in 1527. At this time Henry VIII was looking to cement an alliance with the French and no expense was spared in entertaining the French ambassadors. The huge building measured 110 × 30 feet and was decorated to demonstrate in no uncertain terms the wealth and majesty of the king. The floor area was covered with silk embroidered with gold lilies. The amount of silk needed to make even a lady's gown cost more than many people earned in an entire year, so allowing guests to walk on such rich fabric was a breathtaking symbol of wealth and power. The ceiling was painted to represent the world surrounded by the planets and the signs of the zodiac. It was on this occasion that the void described by Hall took place so that the entertainments were no less impressive than the setting.

Despite its magnificence, though, the banqueting house was really designed to be a shell, rather like the stage in a theatre, which could be redecorated each time it was needed for some important occasion. The fabulous decorations made for it in 1527 were soon removed. Novelty was an important part of royal entertainments and each large-scale event needed a custom-designed setting.[8]

Banqueting houses were by no means always huge, overpowering structures. Banquets could be huge and include large numbers of guests but much more frequently they were small events. Part of the delight of a banquet could be the sense of intimacy, with groups of close friends getting together to enjoy themselves. For this reason many banqueting houses are very small indeed, such as the one built by Sir William Sharington at Lacock Abbey. This is so tiny that it can only hold six or seven people, but it does have access on to the roof of the house and so perhaps it was intended that the company should spill out of the banqueting house to enjoy the view. Sometimes even the Court used much simpler banqueting houses, like the bower in the woods in which 'Robin Hood' entertained Henry VIII and

Katherine of Aragon. Some larger houses were equipped for both types of banquet, having both large banqueting houses and small, intimate ones. Christopher Hatton's house at Holdenby had both types as did Hardwick Hall and Henry VIII's palace at Nonsuch.⁹

Renaissance gardens were supposed to delight the senses, challenge the intellect and refresh the spirit. Banqueting houses formed part of these gardens and so were designed to perform the same functions. One banqueting house intended to stimulate the intellect was Sir Thomas Trensham's famous Triangular Lodge at Rushton in Northamptonshire. Sir Thomas was a Catholic who built the lodge as a banqueting house-cum-prayer room between 1593 and 1596, at a time when it was wise to hide your Catholicism. The symbolism used in the lodge was an expression of his faith. For example, its triangular shape represented the Trinity; it was also a play on Trensham's name.

An excellent way of refreshing the spirit was to ensure a beautiful view from the banqueting house. In the Middle Ages houses had been surrounded by high walls but by the sixteenth century people were feeling confident enough to do away with such security. In Henry VIII's time a banqueting house was even placed on a specially constructed mound by the river at Hampton Court. Thus the diners could look down on the elaborate royal privy garden as well as enjoying views over the river.

The Elizabethans had an even greater passion for views. At Hardwick Hall, for example, a huge expanse of glass was used, and the banqueting house was built up on the roof. This room still has rich decorative plasterwork and, like the Lacock banqueting house, it leads on to the roof, allowing guests to admire the views all around. Sir John Thynne, when building his famous house at Longleat, was not satisfied with a single banqueting house. He had no fewer than four built on his roof. One of them still has the decorative stars on its ceiling which Thynne ordered should be put there. There was also the usual access on to the flat roof to allow guests to wander around and enjoy the views in all directions.

Another way of delighting your guests was to build your house near water. Outdoor banqueting houses were only intended for use during the summer and to take a banquet beside cool water would have been very pleasant indeed. Paul Hentzner recorded his visit to Theobalds, the great house belonging to Lord Burleigh, at the end of the sixteenth century. This is his description of the garden and banqueting house:

. . . one goes into the garden, encompassed with a ditch full of water, large enough for one to have the pleasure of going in a boat, and rowing between the shrubs: there are a great variety of trees and plants, labyrinths made with a great deal of labour, a jet d'eau with its baison of white marble and columns and pyramids of wood and other materials up and down the garden. After seeing these we were led by the gardener into the summer house in the lower part of which, built semicircularly are the twelve Roman emperors in white marble and a table of touchstone,[10] the upper part of it is set round with cisterns of lead, into which the water is conveyed through pipes, so that fish may be kept in them and in summer time they are very convenient for bathing, and another room for entertainment very near this, and jointed to it by a little bridge, was an oval table of red marble.[11]

On a hot day a banquet at Theobalds must have been magical.

Elaborate stone tables like the ones described above were a feature of many banqueting houses. The one at Lacock Abbey still has its magnificently carved table. During the meal the tables were usually covered with fine linen cloths so presumably they would be admired once the food was cleared away.

The Tudors were very concerned that their banquets should include all kinds of novelties, so that the settings for their banquets were designed to be as original as possible. John Parkinson describes what must have been the most unusual banqueting house of its time. This was made out of a huge lime tree which had been trained into a massive three-storey arbour.

And I have seen at Cobham in Kent a tall or great bodied Lime tree, bare without boughes for eight foote high, and then the branches were spread round about so orderly, as if it were done by art, and brought to compose that middle Arbour: And from those boughes the body was bare againe for eight or nine foote (wherein might bee placed halfe an hundred men at the least, as there might likewise in that underneath this) and then another rowe of branches to encompasse a third Arbour, with stayres made for the purpose to this and that underneath it: upon the boughes were laid boards to tread upon which was the goodliest spectacle mine eyes ever beheld for a tree to carry.[12]

Artist's impression of the banqueting house in a lime tree so much admired by John Parkinson.
(Julie Anne Hudson)

In hotter climates banquets might take place not in a banqueting house but in a delightful garden. Cristoforo di Messisbugo worked as maitre d'hôtel at the courts of the dukes of Este in Ferrara at the beginning of the sixteenth century, and later wrote a textbook on banquets and banqueting. He describes several banquets, including one given by Cardinal Hippolyte d'Este for his brother Hercules, Duke of Ferrara. The setting was a beautiful garden, where the table was laid out, covered with three tablecloths. The napkins were elaborately folded into various shapes. The table was covered with rich tableware and sugar figures, which were later replaced by figures made of candied sesame and honey paste. Above the table were festoons of foliage, decorated with various trophies.[13] However, it would be a mistake to imagine the cardinal, in some kind of Arcadian setting, playing at 'getting back to nature' with his guests in the way that people were so fond of doing in the eighteenth century. Sixteenth-century Italian gardens were very elaborate and the garden doubtless owed a great deal more to art than to nature.[14]

The loggias of many famous Italian houses were also very useful for banquets. As they were open at one side, the guests could enjoy the view while still being protected from the heat of the sun and its damaging effects on aristocratic complexions. Many were exquisitely decorated and provided awesome settings for banquets which were impressive even by the high standards of the Renaissance Italian aristocracy.

As usual, the aim was not only to delight the eye but also to display the wealth of the host. One very impressive banquet was served by Agostino Chigi at his magnificent palace in Rome, the Villa Farnesina, in 1518. His principal guest was Pope Leo X. The banquet was held in a loggia overlooking the Tiber and at the end of each course the servants cleared the table by throwing the silver plate into the river. This was not quite the ultimate expression of wealth that it must have appeared. Nets had been hidden in the river to catch the silverware so that it could be recovered later on, after the guests had left. Chigi never revealed this to his guests, though.[15]

Chigi was a man who loved display, as his magnificent villa still shows. At the banquet held to celebrate Chigi's marriage to his mistress Francesca, a ceremony performed by no lesser person than the Pope himself, Chigi presented each diner with a silver plate which had been used during the meal, inscribed with his coat of arms.[16]

Chigi's tableware brings us to another important point about banquets, namely that table settings became so elaborate that they were works of art in themselves. Under the circumstances it was only to be expected that certain tableware would be developed specially for use on such occasions. Firstly, as everything was supposed to be the very best and finest at a banquet, it was very desirable to have glass on the table. The Duke of Rutland's papers record that in 1598 glass plates were hired for serving sweetmeats at dinner, and in 1602 a quantity was bought with 'graven rims' at *6s 2d* per dozen.[17] The glass was used not only for drinking but also for displaying various sweetmeats and jellies, as it showed off their bright colours to best advantage.

The syllabub glass was also much associated with banquets. We think of syllabub today as a solid dessert but originally it was more like a drink, as the cream and the wine were intended to separate. The syllabub would be served in little glass pots with two handles and a spout which came out from the bottom. The wine would be drunk through this spout and then the cream would be eaten with a spoon.[18]

Another item which was often found on the banqueting table was the sucket spoon. This consisted of a spoon with a two-pronged fork at the end of the handle. This was very useful for eating 'wet suckets' (fruit preserved in syrup), as the fork could be used to spear the fruit and then the spoon was for eating the syrup itself. Henry VIII owned sucket spoons, including one made of silver gilt.[19]

Another piece of banqueting tableware was the roundel. These were little wooden plates which were often highly decorated. Many survive today. They are usually round, although a few are rectangular, and are quite small – generally between 12 cm and 14 cm in diameter and only 2–3 mm thick. They were made in sets of eight, twelve or even twenty-four and came in specially made boxes. They were favourite items to give as presents, which perhaps explains why so many sets have the arms of Elizabeth I on the top. This did not mean that they belonged to her, but rather that they were given by her as a gift.

In the late sixteenth and early seventeenth centuries the decoration was not always painted on to the roundel. Instead it was sometimes printed on paper, which was then varnished over.[20] The roundels were not only tableware but also provided entertainment. On one side they might be plain, which was the side intended to be used as a plate. The other side might be decorated with a witty saying, a little

Two examples of the wooden roundels intended for use at banquets, now in the British Museum. Both have verses to recite or sing painted on them. (Copyright British Museum)

poem or even a Bible quotation. This would then be recited or sung by the person who had used the roundel. George Puttenham comments on this custom in *The Arte of English Poesie*, published in 1589. He states that such poems 'neuer contained aboue one verse, or two at the most, but the shorter the better, we call them Posies, and do paint them now a dayes upon the backe sides of our fuirte trenchers of wood'.[21]

These entertainments became so much part of the banquet that little books of witty sayings, poems, songs, etc., were published which included the word 'banquet' in the title. They were not always intended for use at banquets but this does show that the two ideas were linked. An example is *A Banqiet of Daintie Conceits* written by Anthony Munday, which was a collection of lyrics intended to be sung to various well-known tunes of the time.

The entertainments provided at large-scale banquets could be extremely complex and costly, like the ones described in the previous chapter. This scale of entertainment obviously was not appropriate at a small, intimate banquet, where even the grandest people sometimes chose to have very homely and simple games. Cardinal d'Este, at the banquet described earlier, had a farce performed for the delight of his guests, but they also took part in a game of hoop-la. One of Agostino Chigi's banquets, held in honour of Frederico Gonzaga, started with a play, but went on to less formal music and dancing.[22] It would be quite normal, too, for the guests to entertain each other with music, dancing and, of course, witty conversation.

The Elizabethan Court was much influenced by books such as Castiglione's *Courtier*, which first appeared in English translation in

1561. It takes the form of a series of conversations between a group of eminent and sophisticated people at the Court of Urbino. The group discusses what it is that makes the perfect courtier, and one of the skills that is highly praised is that of making good and witty conversation. The true courtier speaks without waffling, is witty without being rude or sarcastic and shows his education by his words. Furthermore good conversation should make everyone feel at ease and the topics should suit everyone's knowledge and tastes.[23] A small, intimate banquet would be just the place for such conversation.

The ideal banquet was therefore very much an expression of all that was considered elegant in the sixteenth century. However, ideals in any century are not always attained, and there was another, darker and much less sophisticated, side to intimate banqueting. In 1583 the puritanical Phillip Stubbes published *The Anatomie of Abuses*, in which he criticizes just about every aspect of Elizabethan society, from eating habits to style of dress. Despite its negative outlook his book does provide a fascinating view of everyday life. Stubbes is distinctly unimpressed with banquets and intimate banqueting houses. Here he complains of the bad behaviour of women in general: 'In the feeldes and Suburbes of the Cities thei have Gardens, either pailed or walled about very high, with their Harbours and Bowers fit for the purpose. And least thei might bee espied in the open places, they have their Banquetting houses with Galleries, Turrettes and what not else therein sumpteously erected, wherein they maie (and doubtesse doe) many of them plaie the filthie persons. . . .'[24] Stubbes, of course, exaggerated greatly, but regarding banquets and banqueting houses, he did have a point. Ever since the Middle Ages walled gardens and intimate bowers had had a close association with lovers and there are many medieval illustrations of 'gardens of love'. Although the upper and middle classes did have more privacy than in the Middle Ages there was still very little privacy by our standards. It was understandable that anyone wanting to be alone with their lover should head for the garden or the banqueting house if there was one.

Certainly banquets provided an opportunity for behaviour which would not have been acceptable on more public occasions. One of the features of the small, intimate banquet was the fact that once the table had been elaborately laid out the serving staff could be dismissed if privacy was wanted. The guests were only really intended to pick at the food anyway, and it was simple enough for the party to serve itself with wine.

According to sixteenth-century medical opinion, the whole menu at a banquet was designed to inflame lust. Wine was a well-known aphrodisiac which 'moveth pleasure and lust of the body', according to Gerard.[25] In addition to wine, 'strong waters', or spirits, were served. These were spirits of wine distilled over various fruits, flowers and so on, and, like many of the other items on the banquet table, were originally regarded as medicines.

Distilling had been very much associated with monasteries, but the Dissolution had brought the skill into the home. By the second half of the sixteenth century every middle- and upper-class lady had her still room, where everything from medicines to cosmetics could be made. It was her task, therefore, to prepare the various 'waters' for the banquet. The range of flavourings was enormous, with all types of herbs and spices being added. Their principal use in the household was still medicinal but with sugar added they were very palatable. Consuming them was also a good way of getting drunk quickly, or at least a quick way of getting to the stage where everyone in the party suddenly seemed very attractive.[26]

According to sixteenth-century thinking, alcohol was not the only item on the banquet table likely to inflame lust. Many other common ingredients of banqueting foods were considered to have the same effect. For example, Gerard mentions aniseed, pine kernels and candied eringo roots (sea holly) – all favourite ingredients. Also considered aphrodisiacs were the various marmalades. Mary Tudor took to eating a special type of marmalade designed to help her to conceive a son. It was full of the very types of food that you would find at a banquet: almonds (thought to encourage fertility), cinnamon, candied eringo roots, candied orange peel, musk, ambergris, cloves and mace.[27] No wonder moralists like Stubbes expected trouble at banquets.

Fresh fruit would also appear on the banquet table when it was in season. Andrew Boorde was of the opinion that figs 'doth stere a man to venryous actes, for they doth auge and increase the sede of generacyoun',[28] so through sixteenth-century eyes even fresh fruit might not have seemed innocent. This is significant as fruit banquets, where fresh fruit rather than sugarwork was served, were a favourite among the middle classes, who would have found too much elaborate banqueting food a strain on their finances.

The very names of some of the items served at banquets also connected them with sex. 'Kissing comfits' made of sugarpaste appear in several recipe books of the time, while 'spannish paps', made of sweetened cream, might also appear at the table.[29] 'Paps' was the sixteenth-century word for breasts. The paps were served in the shape of little mounds, hence their name.

The symbolism of the banquet food sometimes showed a rather obvious link with love and sex too. The sugar figures which decorated the table at Cardinal d'Este's banquet were of Venus, Cupid and Bacchus, the Roman god of wine, well-known characters whose symbolism would have been obvious to all. Evidently the cardinal did not feel that his high position in the Church should lead to a more subtle choice of banquet decoration.

Clearly misbehaviour took place even in the highest circles. The Danish king Christian IV was a famous bon viveur of his day, and is said once to have taken to his bed almost unconscious for two days after over-indulging at a feast. He was the brother-in-law of James I, whose wife was Christian's sister Anne. In 1606 court entertainments were held at Hatfield House in honour of Christian, who was on a visit to England. There were sports and a great feast, followed by a masque about the meeting of King Solomon and the Queen of Sheba. Everyone had over-indulged to such an extent that disaster was inevitable. First, the lady playing the Queen of Sheba fell over in front of Christian and dropped her jewels all over him, causing food to go everywhere. Here is Sir John Harrington's description of what happened next:

> His majesty then got up and would dance with the Queen of Sheba, but he fell down and humbled himself before her, and was carried to an inner chamber and laid in a bed of state, which was not a little defiled with the presents which had been bestowed on his garments; such as wine, cream, jelly, cakes, spices and other good matters. The entertainment and show went forward, and most of the presenters went backwards, or fell down, wine so occupied their upper chambers. Then appeared, in rich dresses, Hope, Faith and Charity. Hope tried to speak, but wine so enfeebled her endeavours, that she withdrew, and hoped the King would excuse her brevity. Faith followed her from the royal presence in a staggering condition. Charity came to the King's feet, and seeming desirous to cover the sins of her sisters, made a sort of obeisance; she brought gifts, but said she would not return home again, as there was no gift which heaven had not already given his majesty; she then returned to Hope and Faith, who were both sick in the lower hall.[30]

King Christian's banquet was hardly the peak of sophistication, but it must definitely have been a night to remember.

Not all of the foods served at a banquet had such a dubious purpose or effect. Certainly they would have been the richest and finest that could be offered at the time. It is worth considering in some detail the types of food which would have been served at an intimate banquet.

This kind of banquet usually happened after the guests had already eaten a large meal. Therefore, it was not intended that the guests should come to the table hungry. The banquet was supposed to tempt what was already a rather jaded palette, and people would pick at it in the way that we might pick at chocolates or mints offered to us after a large meal at a dinner party.

It was even expected that the guests should take some of these delights home with them, as Puttenham talks of 'banketting dishes of sugar plate, or of march paines, and such other dainty meates as by the curtesie and custome every gest might carry from a common feast home with him to his owne house . . .'.[31]

The main ingredient in the food offered was sugar. The use of sugar in this way had developed gradually. Way back in Roman times it had been seen as a medicine rather than a food, and it was possibly the Persians who first used a sweetener. The Arabs then picked up the habit, and it was through contact with the Arabs at the crusades that northern Europeans were introduced to the idea.[32]

For centuries sugar kept its medicinal image. This did not mean that it was not liked – quite the reverse – but it was used with its medical properties in mind. It was seen as a way of helping colds, coughs and lung complaints. This is why various recipes for preserving fruit and flowers in sugar appear in medical manuals rather than recipe books, until the late sixteenth and even early seventeenth centuries. One reason why sugar began to be served after a meal was that it was thought to aid digestion. The practice of coating spices with sugar to make comfits, a favourite banqueting food, came from this same idea.

It was a tradition that making 'banqueting stuffe' was the job of the woman of the house, rather than the cook if there was one. The grandest of households, like the Royal Household, did have full-time confectioners and a separate office of the kitchen devoted to making such things, but the Court was an exception to most rules. Generally in middle- and upper-class households it was the wife's task to produce such work.

This tradition had developed because women were the 'doctors' of the household. Proper, university educated doctors were few and far between and were very expensive. In any case, their education at this time was very theoretical and there were plenty, even among those with money, who mistrusted them.[33] It was the women who were expected to have a knowledge of medicine, including how to make the medicines they used.

As a medicine, sugar naturally came within their sphere. As sugar was also very expensive, most women were probably happier to supervise making preserves and other sugary substances in person. The price of sugar in the early years of the sixteenth century was about 3*d* or 4*d* a pound[34] (which was fairly high considering that a labourer might be living on £2 a year).[35] In the 1540s the price rose to 9*d* or 10*d* a pound and by the 1630s luxury, double-refined sugar was about 30*d* a pound.[36] It is understandable that the sensible housewife should have done the sugarwork herself.

The high price of sugar also made banqueting a very luxurious pastime, and a host who could present his guests with a table laden with sugar delicacies was showing off his wealth in no uncertain terms. One reason why the fashion for this type of banquet food had faded by the eighteenth century was that large-scale sugar plantations had brought the price down to such an extent that it was no longer an exclusive item.

Sugar was an excellent medium for modelling, and parading around sculptures made either of sugar or marchpane (marzipan) was a standard practice at feasts in the Middle Ages. The range of subjects possible was as wide as in any other medium. Models of saints, buildings and statues of the guest of honour all appeared at some time. They were known as 'subtleties' and the more imaginative they were, the better.

To give some impression of just how fabulous these sculptures could be, here is George Cavendish's description of those served by Cardinal Wolsey as part of the entertainment of the French ambassadors in 1527:

> Anon came up the second course with so many dishes, subtletieis and curious devices which were above a hundred in number, of so goodly proportion and costly that I suppose the Frenchmen never saw the like. The wonder was no less that it was worthy indeed. There were castles with images in the same, Paul's Church [St Paul's Cathedral] and steeple in proportion

for the quantity, as well counterfeited as if the painter should have painted it upon a cloth or wall. There were beasts, birds, fowls of divers kinds and personages, most lively made counterfeit in dishes, some fighting, as it were with swords, some with guns and crossbows, some vaulting and leaping, some dancing with ladies, some in complete harness, jousting with spears, and many more devices than I am able with my wit to describe. Among all, one I noted. There was a chessboard subtly made of spiced sweetmeat, with men of the same, and for the good proportion, because Frenchmen be very expert in that play, my lord gave the same to a gentleman of France, commanding that a case should be made for the same in all haste, to preserve it from perishing in the convayance thereof to his country.[37]

The fact that the chessboard was made in honour of the French was very important. These models were sometimes made to flatter the guests and often had considerable political significance. For this reason it was very important that the symbolism should not be lost upon the diners, so mottoes were often attached to the subtleties to explain their meaning. Puttenham remarks on this habit in *The Arte of English Poesie*, noting it as another use for 'poesies'.[38]

Earlier ages had not always valued wit and subtlety in the way that Elizabethans like Puttenham did. For example, the messages at Henry V's wedding feast were certainly to the point. Henry V had, of course, taken France by force and his marriage to the French princess Katherine de Valois was intended to seal his hold on the country. One of the subtleties, which showed an armed man on horseback carrying a tiger cub, bore the motto, in French: 'By force, without cunning, I have taken this beast.' Another of the subtleties presented was more conciliatory. It showed St Katherine surrounded by angels, holding a motto, which said, in French: 'It is written, as is heard and seen, that by a sacred marriage, war shall be terminated.'[39]

The tradition of impressive sugar modelling established by these subtleties was carried on at banquets. Sometimes sugar figures appeared, like the ones of Venus, Cupid and Bacchus at Cardinal d'Este's banquet. Similarly the layout given in John Murrel's *A Delightful Daily Exercise for Ladies and Gentlewomen* shows one or more marchpanes (depending on how you interpret the illustration) on the banquet table, and these would have been made into fancy shapes.[40]

The banquet was intended to be a treat for the eye, so there had to be enormous attention to detail. One impressive centrepiece was not enough. Everything had to be served to its best advantage. Individual sweetmeats would also be highly decorative. The instructions for making sugar plate in *The English Housewife* end with the advice to 'print it at your pleasure'. In other words a mould would be used to make them into fancy shapes.[41] Sir Hugh Platt gives instructions for making a sugar paste 'whereof to cast Rabbets, Pigeons, or any other little birde or beaste, either from the life or carved moulds'.[42]

The art of sugarwork was very advanced in the sixteenth century. Sugar requires a certain amount of skill and patience to work with, even today. In the sixteenth century, before accurate thermometers were available and before sugar could be easily and cheaply bought in different forms, sugarwork must have required the patience of a saint. As confectionery was a necessary accomplishment for a lady she must have taken considerable time learning it in her youth.

Sugar came in large, conical sugar loaves, but it was not necessary to buy a whole loaf at a time. Instead it could be bought by the pound, but it would still have required a great deal of preparation work once it had been brought home. The first stage of using sugar was to refine it. This was a fairly long process, and the instructions given in *The Jewell House of Art and Nature* give some idea of the amount of work involved.

First, a mixture of diluted lime had to be made up, in which as much coarse sugar as the mixture would take was dissolved. This was boiled for a while and then egg whites beaten into oil were added to clarify the mixture. The scum which rose up had to be taken off, and then the clarified liquor was poured through a woollen bag to strain out impurities. The strained liquor had to be boiled up again to evaporate the water, until a thick syrup remained. This syrup was then poured into little moulds, which had holes in the bottom. The sugar would be left to stand overnight with the holes in the moulds stopped up, but the following day the holes would be opened again to allow the molasses to drain out of the white sugar. The final stage of the process, once the sugar had been left to harden until it stopped shrinking in size, was to dry the moulds on a stove. Finally they were wrapped in papers to store them.[43]

Sugar could be bought already refined, but it was very expensive. In the 1630s sugar pieces (taken off a sugar cone with sugar pincers), cost 12*d* a pound, while single refined sugar cost around 22*d* a pound, and double refined sugar about 30*d* a pound.[44]

Once the sugar was refined, you could start to work with it. There were two ways of making the sugar into elaborate shapes. One was to cast the sugar in moulds, as described above, and the other was to make sugar paste, also called sugar plate, which could then be moulded by hand. Here is a recipe written in 1562. The 'Gomme dragante' referred to is gum tragacanth, the resin from an east Mediterranean shrub. This was introduced into England at the end of the fifteenth century and made sugar modelling easier, as it strengthened and bonded the paste.[45]

Take Gomme dragante steeped and tempered in Rose water, until it be soft and whyte, make thereof as it were past, and take of it the bignes of a hasel nut, bray it in a brasen morter, puttinge to it a lyttle poulder of good sugre, and half a graine of fine musk steeped and tempered in Rose water, mire all welle together. And if you wyll have it better, put to it more muske and sugre, and than as much mace beaten in poulder as will lye upon a pennye, and mix it againe well together, than put to it a little of the meale or flower of Amylum [wheat starch] beaten in pouder; but it were better to putte in redde Sandal, wel broken in sonde indifferentelye, and to put it in by litle and lytle, so muche that a manne may make of it a conveniente paste, the whyche you shall cut after your fantasye, and drye it in the shaddowe.[46]

The sugar paste was not always used purely for decoration. Another recipe suggests using paste for 'platters, syshes, glasses, cups and such lyke thinges, wherewith you may furnish a table when you have doen, eate them up. A pleasaunte thing for them that sit at the table.'[47] It was vital to be careful with sugar tableware, though, as a warning is given to 'stand no hot thynge nygh to it'. Heat would have dissolved the sugar. Just in case such tableware was not considered luxury enough, a method of making it 'a thynge of moore finesse' is given. The suggestion is to lay a kind of almond paste between two layers of sugar plate, so that the tableware will taste of almonds.

Casting sugar into different shapes in moulds was another skill a lady needed to learn. Making the moulds themselves was the first step in the process, although it was possible to buy ready-made ones of wood, pewter or even stone. Sir Hugh Platt talks of using wooden moulds, so perhaps these were the most common. Moulds could be made by casting everything from fruit to poultry in plaster of Paris.[48]

Sir Hugh also gives instructions on how to make a plaster mould by casting an object in sand.[49] First of all a wooden platter would be filled with sand and then an object such as a lemon would be pressed halfway down into the sand. The resulting impression was then filled with plaster. Once the plaster was dry it was removed from the sand and then the housewife had the delicate task of scraping the inside of the mould out to make it hollow. She would repeat the whole process so that she was left with two half moulds. These could then be used to cast an entire lemon in sugar.

Evidently the moulds were pretty tricky to use. Sir Hugh starts with advice to dust the moulds with fine powdered sugar, sieved through a piece of lawn or fine linen. The sugar paste is then rolled out with a rolling pin and carefully pressed down into the mould so that it reaches the farthest corners. The mould is then knocked against a table to bring the paste out of the mould. If the mould were a complicated shape this would be a delicate task, and Sir Hugh warns that the gentle use of a knife may be needed to release the paste. It was necessary to work fairly quickly as all the moulding work needed to be complete before the mixture hardened. To make hollow items a more liquid sugar mixture would be used, which had to be carefully swung around to make sure that the sugar coated the whole mould.[50]

It was not enough to present all your sugarwork as white. Ways had to be found to colour at least some of it. Elaborate statues, like the subtleties discussed above, were often painted, but sometimes colour was added to the sugar paste before it was moulded. Making the colours was an art in itself.

Sir Hugh offers advice on how to give sugar paste the colour of violets and other flowers. The flowers were to be heated in a mortar with a little hard sugar, then soaked in rosewater and gum tragacanth, from which the paste was then made.[51] Spices such as cinnamon could also be added to colour the paste, which of course also gave it a particular flavour. Cinnamon would produce a walnut colour, but for a lighter brown Sir Hugh suggests mixing the cinnamon with ginger.[52] Saffron could be used to make yellow, [53] young wheat or barley blades could make a green colour, as could parsley, while carrots could be used to make a 'sanguine colour' (blood red).[54]

It was important to be careful when colouring your sugarwork, particularly if you were intending to use paint. Many paints which gave fashionable, bright colours were definitely not for kitchen use.

One recipe for sugar paste ends with the warning: 'And yf you wylle have it of divers coloures, adde to it suche coloures wele ground as you please. Provided that they be coloures wherein there is no poyson or daunger . . .'.[55]

Cast or moulded sugar, though impressive, was only the tip of the iceberg as far as 'banquetting stuffe' was concerned. All manner of fruit preserved in syrups, fancy sweetmeats, delicate breads and fine butters and cheeses were also required. Another item you would expect to find on the banqueting table was marchpane. This was very like modern almond paste, but not exactly the same. It was made of ground almonds and sugar like our modern version, but usually it was also made with rosewater, and often spices such as cinnamon and nutmeg were added. Again, making it must have been an exercise in patience as the almonds had first to be blanched to remove their skins, then finely ground in a mortar. The sugar had to be 'the finest refined' to start with, and then it had to be sieved through fine linen, which would have given it the texture of modern icing sugar. The paste would usually be shaped or moulded into some elaborate form. Finally, it would be intricately decorated, with icing made of sugar and rosewater, with coloured comfits, or it might even be gilded, and then baked in an oven.[56]

The comfits themselves were quite time consuming to make. Comfits were seeds, spices and even fruits which had been covered with sugar. Sir Hugh gives detailed instructions on making them. The seeds, or whatever was to be sugar coated, were washed and then hung to dry in a brass or lead baison which was suspended over a metal or earthenware pan with hot coals in it. This was to give a low and steady heat. The sugar was put in a pan with a little water and then heated. It was very important to get the temperature right; otherwise, as Sir Hugh warns, the sugar would end up 'black, yellow, or tawny'. Obviously, if the sugarwork was to be served white, it should not be burnt at all. As late as 1750 Dr Johnson observed: 'She should be ashamed to set it before company . . . sweetmeats of so dark a colour as she had often seen at Mistress Sprightly's.'[57] It was for this reason that most delicate sugarwork was done not over the heat of the fire but in a chafing dish set over charcoal, which would be placed upon a table.

The seeds would then be put in small quantities into a ladle and dipped into the sugar. They had to be given several coats of sugar, and had to be dried between each coat. It was a lengthy process. Sir Hugh reckons that in three hours it was possible to make 3 lb of comfits, although this seems to have been if you were working quite quickly.[58] The work involved is even more impressive when you consider that although these comfits were sometimes served alone, more often they were used in the way that we might use hundreds and thousands today, to decorate other sweet items like marchpane.

Another common item found at banquets was a sucket, which might be either wet or dry. Suckets were made from fruit preserved with sugar. The 'wet' ones were those served in syrup, which required the pronged end of a sucket spoon if they were to be eaten politely. The 'dry' suckets were things like marmalades, which were rather different from what we call marmalade today.

Originally marmalade was made from quinces, and was imported from Portugal. The name comes from the Portuguese word for 'quince', which is 'marmelo'. The marmalade was boiled for longer than our version, so that it was fairly solid, and then it was dried in the sun. It was eaten as chunks.[59]

Another favourite dry sucket was preserved lemon or orange peel. Citrus fruits were very expensive imports, so no part of them was wasted. The peels would be boiled in several changes of water to try to remove the bitterness and then they would be preserved in sugar. Andrew Boorde recommended that these should be consumed after dinner to encourage digestion, provided they were eaten 'in succade'.[60]

Wet suckets were many and various. They could be quinces preserved in thick syrup, for which Markham gives a recipe in *The English Housewife*,[61] or they could be almost any other fruit. Some things which we might find rather unexpected were made into suckets, such as green walnuts and lettuce stalks. Both were recommended by Sir Hugh Platt. Green ginger was also a favourite, being another expensive import and therefore yet another expression of wealth. The Johnson family, who were merchants at the staple of Calais in the mid-sixteenth century, were certainly fond of it, to the extent that John Johnson once spent 10s 2d for '2 1b of green ginger given my mother Chantrell'.[62]

In the second half of the sixteenth century cream started to be eaten in higher circles. At one time it was considered beneath the very grand, although it was always a treat for those lower down the social scale as they needed most of their cream for making into butter. Soon, though, its position had changed, and cream was taking its place on the banqueting table in various forms. One dish which developed was syllabub, mentioned earlier in this chapter. Cream also appeared with various flavourings, like the inevitable sugar, intended just to be eaten with a spoon.

Butter was served in much the same way. The nearest modern equivalent is the brandy or rum butter served with Christmas pudding, but in Tudor England butter was considered a dish in its own right. Certainly it seems that Henry VIII and Katherine of Aragon were both fond of flavoured butter. In the Eltham Ordinances the sample menus laid out for them often finish with 'butter and eggs', which was made by beating egg yolks into cream, heating it, and then straining it through a cloth 'so that the Waye may avoide from it', and then adding rosewater and sugar. This was also called 'yellow butter'; if the left-over egg whites were beaten into cream this was called 'white butter'.[63]

A whole range of fancy biscuits and breads was also associated with banquets. These included gingerbreads, which were rather different from the type we are familiar with today. Tudor gingerbread was much heavier than modern ginger sponge cake. It was far more like a biscuit, rather along the lines of modern gingerbread men. It was sometimes made from stale manchet bread, that is, fine white bread, which was grated up and then put through a sieve. Sometimes it was a variant on marchpane, being based on almond paste. Either way it was much more highly spiced than the modern variety tends to be, and often had quite a kick to it. The recipe given by Sir Hugh Platt in *Delights for Ladies*[64] includes not only ginger but also cinnamon, liquorice and aniseed. As the paste was stiff it was easy to make it into fancy shapes and often, like sugar paste, it was pressed into special moulds. Like other banquet dishes, it was highly decorated: often it was gilded.

Some of the biscuits and biscuit breads which were served were spiced, but others were deliberately left quite bland so that they would compliment all the other rich food. The blander biscuits were also useful for dipping into the flavoured creams and butters.

Sponge cake as we know it today did not exist in the sixteenth century. It requires careful, constant heat – which is easy enough to attain in a modern oven but not in a sixteenth-century one. With a Tudor oven a fire was built inside to heat the brickwork of the oven itself. Once it was hot enough the fire would be raked out and the food cooked by means of the heat radiating from the brick. This gave what is known as a 'falling heat', i.e. it gradually decreases.

The closest the Tudors came to sponge were sponge-like biscuits. These were raised either with eggs, as with Lady Fettiplace's 'bisket bread',⁶⁵ or with yeast. The dough was sometimes boiled before it was baked, as are the 'cracknels' in the recipe given in the *The Good Huswifes Jewell*.⁶⁶ The dough was put into boiling water where it would sink to the bottom and then rise to the top again. After it came to the top it would be taken out, dried and then baked.

You might have thought that making these biscuits was rather easier work than making all the various sugarwork, but this was not necessarily the case. *The Good Huswifes Jewell* includes a recipe for 'fine bisket bread' which requires that the mixture be beaten for two hours.⁶⁷

As banqueting was a fashionable pastime many of the biscuit recipes were given names to indicate that they were the finest and most fashionable available. Sir Hugh Platt has French Bisket, prince bisket, and biskitello to lend an interesting, foreign twist. Italy was very much the trend setter at the time, so many of the recipes have Italian names. *The Secrets of Master Alexis of Piedmont* gives a recipe for 'little Morsels as they use in Naples, an exquisite thing'.⁶⁸ There are also numerous other recipes for 'Naples bisket' in other books. These recipes may indeed have come from Italy, but whether they did or not was beside the point. Even the biscuits, relatively plain compared to the other banqueting riches, had to seem exotic and unusual.

Another item which might appear at a banquet was jelly. In order to make this, calves' feet or shavings of antler horn (called hartshorn) had to be boiled for hours and then clarified. An alternative was to use isinglass, which was a kind of gelatin and came from fish. The jelly could then be flavoured with spices, sugar, wine, etc., and coloured brightly. It was usually served in glasses so that its colours could be shown off to best advantage.

Here is Gervase Markham's recipe for jelly. It gives an idea of the large amount of work involved in creating a dish that today would only take minutes to produce. No doubt, though, Markham's jelly would taste considerably better than a modern packet one:

To make the best jelly, take calves' feet and wash them and scald off the hair as clean as you can get it; then split them and take out the fat and lay them in wate, and shift them: then boil them in fair water until it will jelly, which you shall know by now and then cooling a spoonful of the broth; when it will jelly then strain it, and when it is cold then put in a pint of sack and whole cinnamon and ginger sliced and sugar and a little rose-water, and boil all well together again: then beat the white of an egg and put it into it, and let it have one boil more: then put in a branch of rosemary into the bottom of your jelly bag, and let it run through once or twice, and if you will have it coloured, then put in a little turnsole. Also if you want calves' feet you may make as good jelly if you take the like quantity of isinglass, and so use no calves' feet at all.[69]

Turnsole was another colouring obtained from a plant, the *Chrozophoria tinctoria*, which gave a violet or deep-red colour.

A dish rather similar to jelly was leach. Again this was set with gelatin of one kind or another, but it was also made with almonds, new milk, spices and rosewater. The mixture was then strained to produce something similar to a modern milk jelly but with a much more subtle and interesting flavour.[70]

Preparing for banquets obviously was both expensive and time consuming, but fortunately the work did not have to be done all at once. Much of the 'banquetting stuffe' could be prepared well in advance, and many of the recipes for conserves, comfits and so on explain that the finished product will keep for some time. For example, Sir Hugh Platt assures his readers that his 'Paste of Genua Quinces' will keep all year;[71] so too will his 'gelly of Strawberries, Mulberries, Raspisberries or any such tender fruite'. The preparation of banqueting food was therefore an on-going task, although obviously fruit preservation would have to be done when the fruit was in season. The summer must have been a busy time for the housewife, and working in a hot kitchen for hours at a time must have been hard.

It was possible, too, to buy some of the necessities for banquets. There were professional confectioners and it is understandable that ladies were sometimes happy to use the short cut of buying things in. Sabine Johnson certainly did so when she had the chance. The family tended to buy all their confectionery needs, including sugar, on the Continent rather than in England. Her comfits came from Antwerp and were an expensive purchase at about 1*s* a pound, but no doubt were worth it when the alternative was to spend hours over a hot stove.[72] Such short cuts must have made banquets a bit more enjoyable for the lady of the house.

Notes

Chapter One

1   Petre accounts, quoted from Anne Buck, 'The Clothes of Thomasine Petre, 1555–1559', *Costume Society Journal*, No. 24, 1990

2   The letters of the Johnson family, quoted from Barbara Winchester, *Tudor Family Portrait*, Jonathan Cape, London, 1955, p. 152

3   I am indebted to Tom Campbell, formerly of the Victoria & Albert Museum and now of the Metropolitan Museum in New York, for this information

4   *Tudor Family Portrait*, p. 146

5   William Harrison, *The Description of England*, London, 1587, quoted from John Dover Wilson, *Life in Shakespeare's England*, Pelican Books, 1944, p. 268

6   John Russell, *The Book of Nurture*, published in Dr Furnivall (ed.), *The Babees Book: Medieval Manners for the Young*, Chatto and Windus, 1923, pp. 69–73

7   Taken from the Sumptuary Regulations proclaimed on 31 May 1517, printed in *Statutes of the Realm*, Records Commission 1820–8

8   Taken from Douce MS 55 published in *Two Fifteenth Century Cookbooks*, Early English Text Society, Oxford University Press, 1964, p. 115. The manuscript dates from 1450 but this type of food still seems to have been eaten in Tudor England

9   *The Household Papers of Henry Percy, Ninth Earl of Northumberland (1564–1632)*, Royal Historical Society (ed.), 1962

10   This estimate is preserved in the papers of the Duke of Rutland, published in William Jerdan (ed.), *Original documents illustrating the court and times of Henry VII and Henry VIII selected from the private archives of His Grace the Duke of Rutland*, Camden Society, London, 1842. It is quoted from Joycelyne Gledhill Russell, *The Field of Cloth of Gold*, Routledge and Kegan Paul, 1969

11   M.K. Dale trans. *The Household Book of Dame Alice de Bryene*, Suffolk Institute of Archaeology and History, Paradigm Press, Bungay, Suffolk, 1984

12   *Two Fifteenth Century Cookbooks*, p. 30

13   I am indebted to the curatorial team at the Historic Royal Palaces Agency for this information

14   *Tudor Family Portrait*, p. 104

15   *Two Fifteenth Century Cookbooks*, introduction

16   W. Turner, *The Names of Herbes*, London, 1548, quoted from F.A. Roach, *Cultivated Fruits of Britain*, Basil Blackwell, 1985, p. 191

17   John Gerard, *Herball*, London, 1597, and also the edition revised by Thomas Johnson, published in London, 1633, both quoted in *Cultivated Fruits of Britain*, p. 181

18   John Parkinson, *Paradisi in Sole*, London, 1629, quoted from *Cultivated Fruits of Britain*, p. 85

19 Gervase Markham, *The English Housewife*, Michael R. Best (ed.), McGill-Queens University Press, Kingston and Montreal, 1986, pp. 64–7

20 *The English Housewife*, p. 67

21 Ibid., p. 66

22 I am indebted to the curatorial team at the Historic Royal Palaces Agency for this information

Chapter Two

1 Peter Brears, 'Kitchen Fireplaces and Stoves' in Pamela A. Sambrook and Peter Brears (eds), *The Country House Kitchen*, Sutton Publishing, Stroud, 1996, p. 94

2 For a description of various cob irons see 'Kitchen Fireplaces and Stoves', p. 93

3 Ian H. Goodall, 'Medieval Iron Kitchen Equipment' in *The Medieval Kitchen and Its Equipment*, a synopsis of papers presented to a joint meeting of the Finds Research Group and the Medieval Pottery Research Group, Leeds, September 1987

4 *The English Housewife*, p. 77

5 For more information and a diagram of the copper see Simon Thurley, *The Royal Palaces of Tudor England*, Yale University Press, 1993, p. 154

6 'Kitchen Fireplaces and Stoves', p. 101

7 John Murrell, *Two Books of Cookerie and Carving*, Jacksons of Ilkley (facsimile of 1638 edition), 1985, pp. 90, 91

8 Stuart Peachey, *Cooking Techniques and Equipment 1580–1660*, Stuart Press, Bristol, 1994, vol. 1, p. 39

9 *The English Housewife*, p. 83

10 *Three Fifteenth Century Cookbooks*, Thomas Austin (ed.), Early English Text Society, 1964, p. 39

11 S. Minwell Tibbott, *Cooking on the Open Hearth*, National Museum of Wales (Welsh Folk Museum), Cardiff, 1982, p. 11

12 *The English Housewife*, p. 93

13 *Cooking on the Open Hearth*, p. 23

14 *The English Housewife*, p. 83

15 Ibid., pp. 87–8

16 *Cooking on the Open Hearth*, p. 31

17 See 'Kitchen Fireplaces and Stoves', pp. 95–6, for more information

18 The Eltham Ordinances in *A Collection of Ordinances and Regulations for the Government of the Royal Household*, London Society of Antiquaries, London, 1790, p. 218

19 *The English Housewife*, p. 117

20 Ibid., p. 97

21 Ibid., p. 96

22 *The Royal Palaces of Tudor England*, p. 154

23 *A Collection of Ordinances and Regulations for the Government of the Royal Household*, p. 226

24 *The Royal Palaces of Tudor England*, p. 156

25 Andrew Boorde, *A Dyetary of Health*, F.J. Furnivall (ed.), Kegan Paul, Trench and Truber, 1870, p. 239

26 For more information on medieval kitchens see Margaret Wood, *The English Medieval House*, Bracken Books, London, 1965, chapter 17

27 For more information see Peter Brears, 'Behind the Green Baize Door' in *The Country House Kitchen*, p. 37

28 *A Dyetary of Health*, p. 237

29 For a copy of this plan see Madeleine Pelner Cosman, *Fabulous Feasts*, George Braziller, New York, 1976, p. 96

30 *The Royal Palaces of Tudor England*, p. 166

31 Colin Platt, *Medieval Southampton, the Port and Trading Communit AD 1000–1600*, Routledge and Kegan Paul, London, 1973, p. 65

32 Ibid., p. 181

33 Christopher Hereward, 'The Great Trinity Conduit', *Cambridgeshire, Huntingdon and Peterborough Life*, February 1973

34 There is a copy of this broadside in the Guildhall Library, London

35 *A Dyetary of Health*, p. 239

36 *Medieval Southampton*, p. 182

37 Dorothy Hartley, *Water in England*, MacDonald & Co., London, 1964, pp. 346–8

Chapter Three

1 *The Royal Palaces of Tudor England*, p. 153

2 Sue Wright, 'Charmaids, Huswyfes and Hucksters: The Employment of Women in Tudor and Stuart Salisbury', in Lindsay Charles and Lorna Duffin (eds), *Women and Work in Pre-Industrial England*, Croom Helm, 1985, p. 153

3 F.G. Emmison, *Tudor Secretary Sir William Petre at Court and Home*, Longman, 1961, p. 152

4 Ibid., p. 157

5 Hilary Spurling (ed.), *Elinor Fettiplace's Receipt Book*, Penguin, London, 1986, p. 64

6 David Loades, *The Tudor Court*, Headstart History, 1992, p. 65

7 Ibid. See chapter entitled 'The Institutions' for an overview of how the Court was financed and organized

8 *A Collection of Ordinances and Regulations for the Government of the Royal Household*, p. 177

9 *Tudor Secretary Sir William Petre at Court and Home*, p. 127

10 *The Tudor Court*, p. 65

11 *The Royal Palaces of Tudor England*, p. 157

12 Joycelyne Gledhill-Russell, *The Field of Cloth of Gold*, Routledge and Kegan Paul, London, 1969, p. 40

13 Ibid., p. 144

14 Ibid., p. 152

15 *A Collection of Ordinances and Regulations for the Government of the Royal Household*, p. 177

16 *Charmaids, Huswyfes and Hucksters*, p. 104

17 *A Collection of Ordinances and Regulations for the Government of the Royal Household*, p. 148

18 *The Tudor Court*, p. 66

19 Books on domestic service often include information on perquisites but usually concentrate on the eighteenth and nineteenth centuries. For information on that period see the introduction to Samuel and Sarah Adams, *The Complete Servant*, Southover Press, 1989, or Jennifer Davies, *The Victorian Kitchen*, Guild Publishing, London, pp. 32–3

20 *A Collection of Ordinances and Regulations for the Government of the Royal Household*, p. 296

21 Ibid., p. 154

22 *Tudor Secretary Sir William Petre at Court and Home*, p. 137
23 *The Royal Palaces of Tudor England*, p. 150
24 *Tudor Secretary Sir William Petre at Court and Home*, pp. 135, 138
25 Ibid., pp. 132, 151
26 *The Tudor Court*, pp. 68–72
27 *A Collection of Ordinances and Regulations for the Government of the Royal Household*, p. 140
28 See the chapter entitled 'The Pleasures of the Table' in *Tudor Family Portrait*
29 *Tudor Secretary Sir William Petre at Court and Home*, p. 146
30 *Tudor Family Portrait*, p. 132
31 BL Add. MS 7099
32 Joyce Youings, *Sixteenth Century England*, Penguin Books, London, 1984, p. 261

Chapter Four

1 *The English Housewife*, p. 204
2 Andrew Boorde, *A Compendyous Regyment or A Dyetary of Health*, London, 1906, p. 252
3 Sir Thomas Elyot, *The Castel of Helth*, London, 1541, p. 31
4 Peter Clarke, *The English Alehouse: A Social History*, Longman, London and New York, 1983, p. 113
5 Andre L. Simon, *The History of the Wine Trade in England*, Wyman & Sons, London, 1906, vol. II, pp. 162–3
6 William Harrison, *The Description of England*, Constable and Co., London, 1994, p. 113
7 Ibid., p. 247
8 Sir Hugh Platt, *The Jewell House of Art and Nature*, London, 1594, p. 69
9 Compare with William Harrison's comments on drinking habits quoted on pp. 107–9
10 William Benchley Rye, *England as Seen by Foreigners*, John Russell Smith, London, 1865, p. 109
11 *The English Housewife*, pp. 180–98
12 Thomas Tusser, *Five Hundred Points of Good Husbandry*, Oxford University Press, Oxford, 1984, p. 167
13 *The English Housewife*, pp. 204–11
14 *A Compendyous Regyment or A Dyetary of Health*, p. 256
15 Charles Lethbridge Kingsford, *Two London Chronicles from the Collection of John Stow*, edited for the Royal Historical Society, London, Camden Miscellany, 1910, vol. XII, p. 48
16 *The Jewell House of Art and Nature*, pp. 15–17
17 *The Description of England*, p. 131
18 *The Jewell House of Art and Nature*, p. 60
19 *The Description of England*, p. 137
20 Pamela Sambrook, *Country House Brewing*, Ohio Hambledon Press, London and Rio Grande, 1996, p. 22
21 Ibid., p. 23
22 See Peter Clarke, *The English Alehouse: A Social History*. This book gives a good overview of the history of alehouses
23 *The Poetical Works of John Skelton*, Revd Alexander Dyce (ed.), Thomas Rudd, London, vol. I, 1843, p. 95
24 *The Description of England*, p. 116

25   *The Household Book of the Earls of Northumberland*, A. Brown, London, 1905
26   *The English Housewife*, p. 205
27   *Country House Brewing*, p. 139
28   Ibid., p. 108
29   *The English Housewife*, p. 103
30   *The English Alehouse: A Social History*, p. 103
31   *The Household Book of the Earls of Northumberland*, p. 136
32   *Tudor Family Portrait*, pp. 132–3
33   *The Jewell House of Art and Nature*, p. 59
34   *The English Alehouse: A Social History*, p. 100
35   Ibid., p. 97

Chapter Five

1   *The Castel of Helth*, p. 35
2   William Benchley Rye, *England as Seen by Foreigners*, John Russell Smith, London, 1865, p. 52
3   *The History of the Wine Trade in England*, p. 44
4   Thomas Hill, *The Gardener's Labyrinth*, Oxford University Press, Oxford, 1987. There are notes on vines throughout the book but especially on p. 43
5   The clerks of the Brevements were responsible for supervising the distribution of food, etc.
6   *The Household Books of the Earls of Northumberland*, p. 59
7   Hugh Johnson, *The Story of Wine*, Mandarin, London, 1989, p. 126
8   *The History of the Wine Trade in England*, p. 130
9   Ibid., pp. 255–91 show a table of wine prices throughout the sixteenth century
10   Ibid., p. 32
11   *The English Housewife*, p. 142
12   *The History of the Wine Trade in England*, p. 98
13   Ibid., pp. 164–5
14   Ibid., p. 166
15   Ibid., p. 48
16   Ibid., p. 139
17   *The Story of Wine*, p. 124
18   Ibid., p. 125
19   Ibid., p. 127
20   Arnald of Villanova, *The Earliest Printed Book on Wine*, trans. E. Sigerist, Schuman's, New York, 1943, p. 25
21   Ibid., p. 21
22   *The Jewell House of Art and Nature*, p. 64
23   *The English Housewife*, p. 144
24   *The Earliest Printed Book on Wine*, p. 27, and Petrus de Crescentiis, *Le Quatrième Livre du Rustican consacré a la Vigne, à sa culture et à son produit*, Dijon, 1864, pp. 60–1
25   Ibid., p. 27
26   *The Jewell House of Art and Nature*, p. 67
27   Ibid., pp. 65–6
28   *The History of the Wine Trade in England*, p. 165
29   *The Story of Wine*, p. 160
30   *The History of the Wine Trade in England*, p. 273
31   Ibid., p. 44

32   *The English Housewife*, p. 118

33   *The Jewell House of Art and Nature*, p. 65

34   *The History of the Wine Trade in England*, p. 249

35   *The Description of England*, p. 435

Chapter Six

1   For more information on this subject see Andrew B. Appleby, 'Nutrition and Disease: The Case of London 1550–1750' in *Journal of Interdisciplinary History VI: 1*, summer 1975, pp. 1–22

2   For more information on this subject and on the general problems of studying nutrition in history see Massimo Livi-Bacci, *Population and Nutrition*, Cambridge University Press, Cambridge, 1991

3   'Births, Marriages and Deaths: The Recovery of the English Population Record since the Close of the Middle Ages' in Peter Laslett, *The World We Have Lost*, Methuen, London, 1983

4   See 'Did the Peasants Really Starve? Famine and Pestilence among English People in the Pre-industrial Past' in *The World We Have Lost*. For a specific commentary on the famine in Westmorland and Cumberland see Andrew B. Appleby, *Famine in Tudor and Stuart England*, Liverpool University Press, Liverpool, 1978

5   *Population and Nutrition*, p. 87

6   *A Dyetary of Health*, p. 265

7   For a summary of diet and nutrition in the Middle Ages/sixteenth century see J.C. Drummond and Anne Wilbraham, *The Englishman's Food*, Jonathan Cape, London, 1957

8   Ibid., p. 68

9   *Tudor Family Portrait*, p. 142

10   *The Castel of Helth*, p. 36

11   Jacques Guillemeau, *Childbirth, or the Happy Deliverie of Women*, London, 1612, p. 24

12   For more information on food adulteration see Frederick A. Filby, *A History of Food Adulteration and Analysis*, George Allen and Unwin, London, 1934

13   Quoted from *A History of Food Adulteration and Analysis*, pp. 74–5

14   *A Dyetary of Health*, pp. 260–1

15   Furnivall's footnotes to Boorde's *Dyetary of Health* quote Sir John Shene's *Regiam Majestatem* which talks of Scottish brewsters being either fined or ducked for producing bad ale, while their ale was distributed free to the poor

16   *A History of Food Adulteration and Analysis*, p. 29

17   *The Castel of Helth*, p. 13

18   *The Englishman's Food*, p. 86

19   Charles Singer and E. Ashworth, *A Short History of Medicine*, Clarendon Press, 1962, pp. 46–7

20   *The Castel of Helth*, p. 4

21   W.S.C. Copeman, *Diet and Disease in Tudor Times*, Dawson's, 1960, p. 35

22   For more information on the position of women in medicine see Alison Sim, *The Tudor Housewife*, Sutton Publishing, Stroud, 1996

23   William Bulleyn, *The Government of Health*, London, 1558, pp. xxiii–xxviii

24   *The Castel of Helth*, p. 13

25   Ibid., p. 10

26   *A Dyetary of Health*, p. 288

27 *The Government of Health*, p. xviii

28 John Gerard, *The Herball, or General History of Plants* (1633), Dover Publications, New York, 1975, pp. 1452, 1508

29 *The Castel of Helth*, p. 19

30 For more information and comments on what the Tudors thought about ale and beer see chapter four

31 *A Dyetary of Health*, p. 268

32 Thomas Cogan, *The Haven of Health*, London, 1584, p. 157

33 *The Castel of Helth*, pp. 25, 26

34 *The Haven of Health*, p. 157

35 *A Dyetary of Health*, p. 252

36 *Five Hundred Points of Good Husbandry*, p. 164

37 *A Dyetary of Health*, pp. 277–8

38 Ibid., p. 278

39 Ibid., p. 265

40 *The Haven of Health*, p. 150

41 *The Castel of Helth*, p. 150

42 For Boorde's comments see *A Dyetary of Health,* p. 267. For Cogan's comments see *The Haven of Health*, p. 156

43 *A Dyetary of Health*, pp. 236–7

44 Ibid., pp. 262–3

45 Ibid., pp. 289–90

46 *The Castel of Helth*, p. 94

47 *A Dyetary of Health*, p. 296

48 *The Haven of Health*, pp. 245–60

49 *The Castel of Helth*, p. 65

Chapter Seven

1 Household Ordinances of Henry VIII quoted from David Loades, *The Tudor Court*, Headstart History, Bangor, 1992, p. 63

2 A mark was worth a third of a pound

3 George Cavendish, *Life and Death of Cardinal Wolsey*, Folio Society, London, 1962, p. 101

4 'The Inventory of Archbishop Parker's Goods and Chattels' in *Archaeologia XXX*, p. 25, quoted from Timothy Schroder, *The National Trust Book of English Domestic Silver 1500–1900*, Penguin Books, London, 1988, p. 25

5 *Sixteenth Century England*, 1984, p. 146

6 *The National Trust Book of English Domestic Silver 1500–1900*, p. 20

7 Ibid.

8 Spice plates were so named as they were often used for serving spiced bread

9 *The Description of England*, p. 367

10 Ibid., pp. 366–7

11 C.V. Malfatti, *Two Italian Accounts of Tudor England*, C.V. Malfatti, Barcelona, 1953, p. 32

12 *The Description of England*, p. 202

13 John Hatcher and T.C. Barker, *A History of British Pewter*, Longman, London and New York, 1974, p. 96

14 Peter R.G. Hornsby, Rosemary Weinstein and Ronald F. Homer, *Pewter: A Celebration of the Craft 1200–1700*, The Museum of London, London, 1989, p. 22

15 David Gaimster, 'The Archaeology of Post-Medieval Society *c.* 1450–1750:

Material Culture Studies in Britain since the War' in *Building on the Past: Papers Celebrating 150 years of the Royal Archaeological Institute*, The Royal Archaeological Institute, 1994, and David Gaimster, 'The Supply of Rhenish Stoneware to London 1350–1600', *The London Archaeologist,* vol. 15, no. 13 (winter 1987), pp. 339–47

16   See *The National Trust Book of English Domestic Silver 1500–1900*, p. 42, for more information on the English habit of mounting objects with silver

17   Griselda Lewis, *A Collector's History of English Pottery*, Antique Collectors' Club, 1987, p. 38

18   Philippa Glanville, 'The Company Plate *c.* 1520', *Review of the Worshipful Company of Goldsmiths 1984–5*, p. 20

19   The Camden Society, *The Inventory of the Wardrobe, Plate etc. of Henry Fitzroy, Duke of Richmond and Somerset*, The Camden Miscellany, vol. 3, 1855, pp. 4–5

20   *The Company Plate*, p. 20

21   D. Battle and Simon Cottle (eds), *Sotheby's Concise Encyclopaedia of Glass*, Conran Octopus, London, 1991. For information on sixteenth-century glass see pp. 60–76

22   Ibid., p. 65

23   *The Description of England*, p. 128

24   *Sotheby's Concise Encyclopaedia of Glass*, p. 76

25   Norman Gask, *Old Silver Spoons of England*, Herbert James Ltd, London, 1926. Chapter 8 lists the spoons in the 'Jewel Book' of Henry VIII

26   Thomas Coryat, *Coryat's Crudities*, vol. 1, James Maclehose & Sons, 1791, p. 236

27   *Old Silver Spoons of England*, p. 83

28   *The Company Plate*, p. 21

29   Surtees Society, vol. 26, p. 193, quoted from *The National Trust Book of English Domestic Silver 1500–1900*, p. 85

30   *The National Trust Book of English Domestic Silver 1500–1900*, p. 20

31   Edith Rickert (ed.), *The Babees Book: Medieval Manners for the Young Done into Modern English from Dr Furnivall's Texts*, Chatto and Windus, London, 1923, p. 6

32   *The Inventory of the Wardrobe, Plate etc. of Henry Fitzroy, Duke of Richmond and Somerset*, pp. 9–10

Chapter Eight

1   *The Little Children's Little Book* in *The Babees Book*, p. 18

2   J.K. Sawards (ed.), *De Civilitate Morum Puerilium* in *The Collected Works of Erasmus*, vol. 25. For information on eating see pp. 281–5

3   *The Young Children's Book* in *The Babees Book*, p. 24

4   *The Little Children's Little Book*, p. 18

5   *The Description of England*, p. 127

6   Ibid., p. 128

7   *The Young Children's Book*, p. 25

8   Peter Briers, *Decorating the Tudor and Stuart Table* in C. Anne Wilson (ed.), *The Appetite and the Eye*, Edinburgh University Press, Edinburgh, 1991, p. 75

9   Richard Weste, *The School of Virtue* in *The Babees Book*, p. 174

10   *The Young Children's Book* in *The Babees Book*, p. 25

11   Francis Seager, *School of Virtue* in *The Babees Book*, p. 152

12   Hugh Rhodes, *Book of Nurture* in *The Babees Book*, p. 138

13   John Murrell, *Two Books of Cookerie and Carving*, Jacksons of Ilkley, Ilkley, 1985, pp. 166–73

14   *The Inventory of the Wardrobe, Plate etc. of Henry Fitzroy, Duke of Richmond*, p. 11

15   *The Young Scholar's Paradise* in *The Babees Book*, p. 167

16   *The Book of Courtesy* in *The Babees Book*, p. 83

17   Household Ordinances of Edward IV quoted in the introduction to *The Babees Book*, p. xxv

18   The observations of a German visitor to Elizabeth's Court quoted in the introduction to Revd Richard Warner, *Antiquitates Culinariae*, London, 1791, p. xlv

19   *The English Housewife*, p. 121

20   *School of Virtue* in *The Babees Book*, p. 153

Chapter Nine

1   Donald Attwater, *The Penguin Dictionary of Saints*, second edition, Penguin Books, London, 1983, p. 243

2   Quoted from Frank Sidgwick and E.K. Chambers, *Early English Lyrics*, Sidgwick & Jackson, London, 1966, p. 235

3   *Five Hundred Points of Good Husbandry*, p. 65

4   See the recipe for Three Kings almond tart in Jennifer Paterson and Clarissa Dickson Wright, *Two Fat Ladies*, Ebury Press, London, 1996, p. 80

5   Bridget Ann Henish, *Cakes and Characters*, Prospect Books, London, 1984, p. 39

6   *Cakes and Characters*, chapter 4

7   Joseph Robertson (ed.), *Inventaires de la Royne Descosse Douairiere de France*, Bannatyne Club, Edinburgh, 1863, p. xlix quoted in *Cakes and Characters*, p. 28

8   *A Collection of Ordinances and Regulations for the Government of the Royal Household*, London Society of Antiquaries, London, 1790, p. 120

9   John Stow, *The History and Survey of the Cities of London and Westminster*, London, 1753, p. 234

10   *Elinor Fettiplace's Receipt Book*, p. 114

11   For an example see Thomas Austin (ed.), *Two Fifteenth Century Cookery Books*, Early English Text Society, 1964, p. 70

12   *Five Hundred Points of Good Husbandry*, p. 178

13   Ibid., p. 23

14   Eileen Power (ed.), *The Goodwife of Paris*, George Routledge & Sons, London, 1928, p. 262

15   *A Collection of Ordinances and Regulations*, p. 174

16   Ibid., pp. 177–8

17   *Five Hundred Points of Good Husbandry*, p. 24

18   *The Goodwife of Paris*, p. 283

19   George Cavendish, *The Life and Death of Cardinal Wolsey*, ed. Roger Lockyer, Folio Society, London, 1962, p. 194

20   *A Collection of Ordinances and Regulations*, p. 174

21   William Lambarde, *A Perambulation of Kent*, London, 1596, pp. 246–7

22   F.A. Roach, *Cultivated Fruits of Britain*, Basil Blackwell, Oxford and New York, 1985, p. 30

23   Turner's *Herbal* quoted from *Cultivated Fruits of Britain*, p. 101

24   *The Castel of Helth*, p. 24

25   *A Dyetary of Health*, p. 283

26   *Paradisi in Sole*, p. 582

27   *The English Housewife*, pp. 118–19

28   *The Herbal, or General History of Plants*, p. 1154

29   *Paradisi in Sole*, p. 518

30 Ronald Webber, *The History of Commercial Flower, Fruit and Vegetable Growing*, Newton Abbot, 1972, p. 30

31 *Paradisi in Sole*, p. 518

32 *The Herbal, or General History of Plants*, pp. 926–8

33 *Paradisi in Sole*, p. 518

34 *The English Housewife*, p. 62

35 *The Herbal, or General History of Plants*, p. 346

36 For more information on sugarwork see chapter ten

37 George Cavendish, *Life and Death of Cardinal Wolsey*, London Folio Society, London, 1962, pp. 53–7

38 John Nichols (ed.), *The Progresses and Public Procession of Queen Elizabeth* (1823), Burt Franklin, New York, 1966, vol. III, pp. 140–3, quoted in Bridget Ann Henisch, *Cakes and Characters*, Prospect Books, London, 1984, p. 27

39 For more details of the Field of Cloth of Gold see Joycelyne Gledhill Russell, *The Field of Cloth of Gold*, Routledge and Kegan Paul, London, 1969

40 Edward Hall, *The Triumphant Reigne of Kyng Henry the VIII*, J. Johnson, London, 1809, pp. 606–7

41 Rawdon Brown (ed.), *Calendar of State Papers and Manuscripts Existing in the Archives and Collections of Venice*, vol. 5, 1520–6 2073 (181), Longman's Green, London, 1869, p. 62

42 *The Triumphant Reigne of Kyng Henry the VIII*, p. 612

43 Ibid., p. 614

44 Ibid., p. 514

45 For details on the organization of the Revels Office see Streitberger, *Court Revels*

46 For more information on Elizabeth's public image see Roy Strong, *The Cult of Elizabeth*, Thames & Hudson, London, 1977

47 A. Brown (ed.), *The Northumberland Household Accounts*, London, 1905, p. 103

Chapter Ten

1 For the development of the banquet see C. Anne Wilson, 'The Evolution of the Banquet Course' in C. Anne Wilson (ed.), *Banquetting Stuffe*, Edinburgh University Press, Edinburgh, 1991

2 Eileen Power (ed.), *The Goodwife of Paris*, George Routledge & Sons, London, 1928, p. 238

3 *Ordinances for the Royal Household from Edward III to William and Mary*, Society of Antiquaries, London, 1790, p. 113

4 *The Triumphant Reigne of Kyng Henry the VIII*, p. 595

5 According to William Harrison, a pace, was 5 ft

6 *The Field of Cloth of Gold*, p. 29

7 Ibid., p. 41

8 David Starkey (ed.), *Henry VIII: A European Court in England*, Collins & Brown, London, 1991, pp. 64–6

9 For information on banqueting houses see Jennifer Stead, 'Bowers of Bliss: The Banquet Setting' in *Banquetting Stuffe*

10 Touchstone was stone on which gold and silver left a streak when rubbed against it

11 Paul Hentzner, *A Journey into England*, trans. Horace Walpole, London, 1757, pp. 54–5

12 *Paradisi in Sole*, p. 610

13   The banquet is described in more detail in Michael Jeanneret, *A Feast of Words*, trans. J. Whiteby and Emma Hughes, Polity Press, 1991, p. 51

14   For more information on Italian Renaissance gardens see David R. Coffin, *The Villa in the Life of Renaissance Rome*, Princeton University Press, Princeton, 1979

15   Ibid., p. 108

16   Ibid.

17   Duke of Rutland's MSS quoted from G. Bernard Hughes, *English, Scottish and Irish Table Glass*, B.T. Batsford, London, 1956, p. 285

18   See Peter Brears, 'Rare Conceites and Strange Delightes' in *Banquetting Stuffe*, p. 83

19   The inventory of Henry VIII's jewel house quoted from Norman Gask, *Old Silver Spoons of England*, Herbert Jenkins Ltd, London, 1926

20   Edward H. Pinto, *Treen and Other Wooden Bygones*, G. Bell & Sons, London, 1969, pp. 79–80

21   See chapter thirty, 'Of Short Epigrames called Posies', in George Puttenham, *The Arte of English Poesie* (1589), ed. Gladys Doidge Willcock and Alice Walker Puttenham, Cambridge University Press, Cambridge, 1936, p. 58

22   *The Villa in the Life of Renaissance Rome*, p. 107

23   For more information on the ideals of conversation see *A Feast of Words*, p. 51

24   Phillip Stubbes, *The Anatomie of Abuses*, London, 1583, pp. 48–9

25   *The Herbal, or General History of Plants*, p. 880

26   For more information on strong waters see 'The Evolution of the Banquet Course' in *Banquetting Stuffe*

27   'Bowers of Bliss: The Banquet Setting' in *Banquetting Stuffe*

28   *A Dyetary of Health*, p. 282

29   See 'Rare Conceites and Strange Delightes' in *Banquetting Stuffe*

30   Quoted from Philippa Pullar, *Consuming Passions*, Hamish Hamilton, London, 1970. Unfortunately the book has no footnotes, so I do not know the original source

31   *The Arte of English Poesie*, p. 58

32   For information on the use of sugar in Europe see 'The Evolution of the Banquet Course' in *Banquetting Stuffe*, pp. 16–18

33   For information on women's place in medicine see Alison Sim, *The Tudor Housewife*, Sutton Publishing, Stroud, 1996

34   See the chapter 'Inflation of Population and Prices' in *The Sixteenth Century*

35   'The Evolution of the Banquet Course' in *Banquetting Stuffe*, p. 23

36   Robert and Jane Huggett and Stuart Peachy, *Early Seventeenth Century Prices and Wages*, Stuart Press, Bristol, p. 23

37   *The Life and Death of Cardinal Wolsey*, p. 103

38   *The Arte of English Poesie*, p. 58

39   Revd Richard Warner, *Antiquitates Culinariae*, London, 1791, p. 115

40   A transcription of Murrel's layout can be found in Stuart Peachy, *Feast and Banquet Menus*, Stuart Press, Bristol, 1992

41   *The English Housewife*, p. 115

42   Sir Hugh Platt, *Delightes for Ladies*, Crosby, Lockwood & Son, 1948, p. 23

43   *The Jewell House of Art and Nature*, pp. 94–6

44   *Early Seventeenth Century Prices and Wages*, p. 23

45   'The Evolution of the Banquet Course' in *Banquetting Stuffe*, p. 20

46   Wyllyam Warde trans., *The Secrets of the Reverende Master Alexis of Piedmont*, London, 1562, p. 53

47   Ibid., p. 64

48   Anyone who wants to try sugarwork for themselves should see Peter Brears, 'Rare Conceites and Strange Delightes' in *Banquetting Stuffe*

49   *Delightes for Ladies*, p. 38

50   Ibid., pp. 38–9

51   Ibid., p. 27

52   Ibid., p. 35

53   Ibid., p. 38

54   Rosselli, *Epilario, or the Italian Banquet*, London, 1598, section K

55   *The Secrets of the Reverende Master Alexis of Piedmont*, p. 53

56   *The English Housewife*, p. 116

57   Quoted from 'Bowers of Bliss: The Banquet Setting' in *Banquetting Stuffe*, p. 143

58   *Delightes for Ladies*, p. 44

59   'The Evolution of the Banquet Course' in *Banquetting Stuffe*, pp. 22–5

60   *A Dyetary of Health*, p. 286

61   *The English Housewife*, p. 111

62   *Tudor Family Portrait*, p. 142

63   Thomas Dawson, *The Good Huswifes Jewell*, London, 1596/7, book 2, p. 20

64   *Delightes for Ladies*, p. 29

65   *The Complete Receipt Book of Ladie Elynor Fetiplace*, Stuart Press, Bristol, 1994, vol. 1, p. 45

66   *The Good Huswifes Jewell*, p. 12

67   Ibid., p. 13

68   *The Secrets of the Reverende Master Alexis of Piedmont*, p. 66

69   *The English Housewife*, p. 41

70   Ibid., p. 111

71   *Delightes for Ladies*, p. 33

72   *Tudor Family Portrait*, p. 142

Further Reading

For general information on life in the sixteenth century:

Georges Edelen and William Harrison (eds), *The Description of England*, The Folger Shakespeare Library and Dover Books, 1994

F.G. Emmison, *Tudor Secretary: Sir William Petre at Court and Home*, Longmans, 1961

Barbara Winchester, *Tudor Family Portrait*, Jonathan Cape, 1955

Joyce Youings, *Sixteenth Century England*, Penguin Books, 1988

For information on the Tudor Court, how it was organized and what it was like to live in:

David Loades, *The Tudor Court*, Headstart History, 1992

Roger Lockyer (ed.), George Cavendish, *The Life and Death of Cardinal Wolsey,* Folio Society, 1962

Muriel St-Clare Byrne, *The Lisle Letters*, Penguin Books, 1982

Simon Thurley, *The Royal Palaces of Tudor England*, Yale University, 1993

Anyone with an interest in Tudor royal entertainments and their political significance should try:

Joycelyne Gledhill Russell, *The Field of Cloth of Gold*, Routledge and Kegan Paul, 1969

W.R. Streitberger, *Court Revels 1485–1559*, University of Toronto Press, 1994

Roy Strong, *The Cult of Elizabeth*, Thames and Hudson, 1977

For an overview of the history of English food:

Maggie Black et al., *A Taste of History*, English Heritage in association with the British Museum Press, 1993

J.C. Drummond and Anne Wilbraham, *The Englishman's Food*, Jonathan Cape, 1957

Madeleine Pelner Cosman, *Fabulous Feasts,* George Braziller, 1976 (reprinted 1992)

C. Anne Wilson, *Food and Drink in Britain*, Constable and Co.

For information on kitchens:

Pamela A. Sambrook and Peter Brears (eds), *The Country House Kitchen 1650–1900*, Sutton Publishing in association with the National Trust, 1996

Margaret Wood, *The English Mediaeval House*, Bracken Books, 1965 (reprinted 1990)

Simon Thurley's *The Royal Palaces of Tudor England* also contains an interesting section on the palace kitchens.

For information on Tudor medicine:

W.S.C. Copeman, *Doctors and Disease in Tudor Times*, Dawson, 1960

Charles Singer and E. Ashworth, *A Short History of Medicine*, Clarendon Press, 1962

Unfortunately, even the reprints of the health manuals of the day are now rather difficult to obtain. Anyone with an interest in them needs access to a very good library.

Various sixteenth- and seventeenth-century cookery books and household manuals are now available in modern versions. Here are a few suggestions:

Michael R. Best (ed.), *The English Housewife*, McGill-Queen's University Press, 1986

Hilary Spurling (ed.), *Elinor Fettiplace's Receipt Book*, Penguin Books, 1986

Thomas Tusser, *Five Hundred Points of Good Husbandry*, Oxford University Press, 1984

Index